CONVERSATION
WITH CHRIST

PETER ROHRBACH

CONVERSATION WITH CHRIST

TAN Books and Publishers, Inc.
Rockford, Illinois

Nihil obstat: Robert S. Pelton, C.S.C.
               Censor Deputatus

Imprimatur: ✠ Leo A. Pursley, D.D.,
               Apostolic Administrator of the
                 Diocese of Fort Wayne, Indiana
               20 April 1956

Originally published in 1956 by Fides Publishers, Chicago, Illinois and later reprinted by Fides in conjunction with Our Sunday Visitor. Reprinted with the present preface in 1980 by Four Courts Press, Dublin, Ireland. The present printing is taken from the Four Courts Press edition.

ISBN: 0-89555-180-2

Printed and bound in the United States of America.

TAN Books and Publishers, Inc.
P.O. Box 424
Rockford, Illinois 61105

1982

TO

OUR LADY OF MOUNT CARMEL—

WHO WATCHES OVER US WITH EXQUISITE TENDERNESS,

GUIDES US WITH UNERRING PRECISION, AND PROCURES

FOR US MYRIAD HAPPINESS—

THIS BOOK IS AFFECTIONATELY AND

GRATEFULLY DEDICATED

Do not be astonished at the difficulties one meets in the way of mental prayer, and the many things to be considered in undertaking this heavenly journey. The road upon which we enter is a royal highway which leads to heaven. Is it strange that the attainment of such a treasure should cost us something? The time will come when we shall realize that the whole world could not purchase it.

—St. Teresa of Avila

PREFACE TO THE 1980 EDITION

The world has changed in many ways since the initial publication of this book, but the fact that it continues to be published in edition after edition over the years suggests that there might very well be something quite changeless about what the book discusses.

Conversation with Christ is an attempt to explain and outline St. Teresa of Avila's teaching about personal prayer, first described by her so lucidly in her 16th century writings. Indeed, since the initial publication of this book, St. Teresa has been declared a Doctor of the Church, which is yet another testament to the validity and permanence of her teaching. However, her teaching about prayer is not something unique in the history of Christianity, a private and recondite doctrine, but rather it is an explanation of the basic doctrine about prayer as expressed in the pages of Scripture.

In the earliest pages of Scripture God is presented to us as a *person*, and as a person who desires to establish a relationship with his creatures. The primary vehicle of that relationship, as outlined in Scripture, was prayer, and the long biblical narrative is a continuing account of mankind's attempt to remain in faithful association with his God. The psalms, for instance, are a factual reportage of the ancient Jews' prayers to God, demonstrating how those early believers worshipped Yahweh, how they expressed their gratitude to him, how they sought his assistance, and how they evidenced their love for him.

Jesus, entering the scene of human history, continued to emphasise that vital necessity of prayer for an authentic religious life, both in his teaching and in the practical example of his life. In the few years of his public ministry, Jesus was involved in an extremely active life, teaching and healing and laying the foundations of Christianity, but he was simultaneously a dedicated man of prayer. We see him stealing away from the crowds to give himself to private prayer, even spending whole nights in prayer or rising early before his disciples to pray alone. He taught his disciples the Lord's Prayer, and he frequently commented on the value and the efficacy of prayer. "But when you pray, go to your private room," he said, "and when you have shut the door pray to your Father in the secret place."

What St. Teresa has done so brilliantly is to describe precisely *how* a person can indeed contact God through prayer. Despite her reputation as a soaring Spanish mystic, she was an eminently practical person, and that practicality shines through her teachings about prayer: she is an instructor who shows, in step-by-step fashion, how the individual can contact God and then sustain that relationship.

It is also important to note that St. Teresa argues for the necessity of both private and liturgical prayer. And, again, this represents fidelity to the scriptural message: Jesus was a man of private prayer, but he also prayed publicly with his disciples, particularly at the Last Supper. This is a critical point to note today when there seems to be a lessening enthusiasm in some quarters for what we call mental or private prayer. Vatican Council II addressed that question sharply in the *Constitution on the Sacred Liturgy* when it stated: "The spiritual life, however, is not confined to participation in the liturgy. The Christian is assuredly called to pray with his brethren, but he must also enter into his secret chamber to pray to the Father in secret."

As a matter of fact, St. Teresa chided at a fundamental distinction between private and public prayer: for her, all prayer should entail contact with God, and if any form of public prayer did not involve that contact then it was not, in her terms, prayer. Her teaching, therefore, tells us how to contact God, whether it is expressed privately or in communion with others. More modern religious authors have termed this experience "an effort of conscious communication with God." Teresa of Avila, in a now classic phrase of religious literature, called it a *conversation with Christ*. And she shows us the way to achieve it.

Peter Thomas Rohrbach

15 January 1980

CONTENTS

Contents

Part IV. Difficulties in Meditation

Part V. Demonstration of the Method

Part VI. Indispensable Aids to Meditation

Part VII. Progress in Meditation

Part VIII. The Royal Highway

I

The Nature
of Meditation

"Prayer is . . . conversation with Him."

—St. Teresa

CHAPTER

1

THE PURPOSE
OF MEDITATION

A GOOD DEAL of the confusion surrounding meditation
results from a failure to recognize its basic, fundamental purpose. Simply stated, the aim of meditation
is to provide a framework or setting for a personal,
heart-to-heart conversation with Christ. If this primary
goal is retained in mind throughout our entire discussion
of meditation, much of the mystery will fade away.

St. Teresa sums up the whole matter with one magnificent sweep of the pen in her classical definition of
mental prayer:

> Mental prayer is nothing else than an intimate friendship, a
> frequent heart-to-heart conversation with Him by whom we
> know ourselves to be loved.[1]

Therefore, all that precedes meditation, all that ac-
companies it, and all that follows it, has for its primary
aim the stimulation of this conversation with Christ.

[1] St. Teresa, *Life*, viii.

3

Let us repeat it again—for it is of extreme importance—meditation, in its final analysis, should be basically a friendly conversation with Christ.

The practice of meditation has assumed frightening proportions in the minds of many. It is regarded warily as some type of mental workout which leaves one better prepared to serve God, a spiritual "setting-up exercise." The assumption, therefore, is that meditation is intended only for intellectuals, and is definitely not something to be undertaken rashly by those further down the intellectual ladder. Nothing could be further from the truth; meditation is for all, university professors, and grade school graduates alike.

First of all, the word "meditation." The term is confusing; for in this conversation with Christ, meditation is only one part of the process. By entitling the entire procedure "meditation," we are in effect calling the whole by one of its parts. St. Teresa preferred to designate the process "mental prayer," and in her writings one finds the terms "mental prayer" and "prayer" predominantly employed in place of "meditation." But to preclude further difficulty, we will continue to designate the entire process by the more widely accepted term "meditation," with the tacit reservation that meditation is but one of the divisions of mental prayer. In following this pattern, we will here employ the word "consideration" for that part of prayer which is specifically the meditation.

Meditation, then, is interior prayer without the aid of rosaries, prayer books, or missals. It is the prayer in which we talk to God in our own words. It is distinguished from vocal prayer which employs the words and sentiments of some saint, spiritual writer, or the liturgy itself.

St. Teresa rather chides at the sharp distinction made between mental and vocal prayer. The erroneous assumption in many quarters is that conversation with God is the aim of mental prayer, but not of vocal prayer. St. Teresa is vigorous in her assertion that we must talk to God in both mental and vocal prayer. Vocal prayer, she staunchly maintains, in which interior contact with God is absent, is no prayer at all.[2] During vocal prayer we rely on the formulae of some other person; in mental prayer we attempt to stimulate a direct conversation with Christ using our own words and thoughts.

While it is important to remember what meditation *is*, it is equally important to remember what it is *not*. It is definitely not spiritual reading, nor examination of conscience, nor the formation of rules for better conduct.

Modern methods have lent to the general confusion by attempting to cram spiritual reading, examination of conscience, and amendment of life into the period of meditation. These practices have a definite position of importance in the spiritual life; but that position is not the period of meditation.

Spiritual reading is quite necessary in our times to

---

[2] "I do not allude to mental prayer more than to vocal prayer. For, if it is to be prayer at all, the mind must take a part in it. If a person neither considers whom he is addressing, what he asks, nor what he himself is who ventures to speak to God, although his lips may move with many words, I do not call it prayer." St. Teresa, *Interior Mansion*, I, i.

center our hearts on the true purpose of life in face of the unrelenting media which constantly channel a materialistic philosophy of living into our lives and homes. But this is an exercise distinct from prayer. It is also imperative that we examine our consciences daily if progress in virtue is to be made. Concomitant with this should be the formation of definite resolutions for the future. But again, these are not the primary functions of meditation. Meditation is conversation with Christ, and our talk with Him will often conclude with a promise to be more faithful in the future. This, however, is something that flows from our conversation; it is not a necessary part of it, for it may or may not be present on different occasions.

In employing the term "conversation," St. Teresa, of course, does not intend to infer that it is requisite to formulate explicit words interiorly—although this is advisable for those beginning the practice of meditation. The habit of meditation should bring us into loving contact with Christ, and our affection for Him may be expressed with or without words. At times it will be entirely proper to remain in Christ's presence as did the apostles on Mount Thabor—"Lord, it is good for us to be here." [3] Our affection for Christ may be manifested in a loving "gaze" upon Him; or in any number of wordless expressions of our love for Him. All of these forms of contact are included in the phrase "conversation with Christ."

Nor is meditation limited to contact with Christ alone. We may hold our conversation with God, our

---

[3] Luke 9, 33.

loving Father, or with the Blessed Mother, or any of the saints. But to simplify our discussion, we shall continue to speak throughout of conversation with Christ.

But at the outset, let us remember the fundamental aim of meditation as proposed by St. Teresa: the attainment of a friendly, intimate conversation with Christ. If this be retained in mind throughout, a giant step will have been taken along the road to successful meditation.

2

THE NECESSITY
OF MEDITATION

BEFORE EMBARKING on our discussion of the practice of mental prayer, it would be well to pause and examine the motive for meditating. Why do spiritual writers place so much insistence upon the practice of meditation? Is it an integral part of the spiritual life; or is it a superfluous nicety of spiritual esthetes?

To answer the question let us call on two saints of the Church, St. Alphonsus and St. Teresa. St. Alphonsus stoutly maintains:

It is morally impossible for him who neglects meditation to live without sin.[1]

St. Teresa corroborates his statement in these words:

He who neglects mental prayer needs not a devil to carry him to hell, but he brings himself there with his own hands.[2]

---

[1] St. Alphonsus Liguori, *The Great Means of Salvation and Perfection* (Brooklyn: Redemptorist Fathers, 1927), p. 257.
[2] Quoted by St. Alphonsus, *op. cit.*, p. 256.

We can readily ascertain that meditation in the mind of these two saints is no superfluous nicety, it is a basic necessity for spiritual living. Nor is this insistence on mental prayer merely a pet theory of theirs. They reflect the traditional doctrine of the Church.

In our own day, Pope Pius XII has paused twice in his encyclicals to remind us of the value of meditation:

> Moreover, the common practice of the Saints as well as ecclesiastical documents demonstrate how highly everyone should esteem mental prayer.[3]

> It must be stated without reservation that no other means has the unique efficacy of meditation, and that as a consequent, its daily practice can in no wise be substituted for.[4]

The case for meditation can be easily proved. Christ came to earth to re-establish God's friendship with man— "I call you now not servants, but friends." [5] Our Lord Himself has made the initial overture in this friendship; we must, on our part, reciprocate, and strive to maintain the companionship at its highest level. This entails a sustained contact with Christ; and prayer is our principal contact with Him. However, vocal prayer does not completely fulfill this need—we are required to employ the language of the Church's official prayers, but we must also converse with God in sentiments which arise from our own hearts and are expressed in our own words. As St. Teresa comments:

> Take my advice and let no one mislead you by pointing out any other way than prayer. I am not discussing here whether

---

[3] Pius XII, *Mystici Corporis*. (No. 105 in America Press Edition)
[4] Pius XII. *Menti Nostrae*. (No. 47 in NCWC Edition)
[5] St. John, 15, 15.

mental and vocal prayer are necessary for everybody; but I contend that you require both.[6]

There is serious danger in restricting our prayer life to vocal prayer: we stand the risk of becoming victims of that vicious habit of sing-songing our prayers without actually contacting Christ. Furthermore, the true lover wishes to express his affection in his own words, and not rely on the "canned" sentiments of a spiritual writer. In meditation the soul is forced, as it were, to speak directly with Christ; there can be no hiding behind standardized formulae of prayer. And this is the way the truly spiritual man would want it: an opportunity to speak privately with Christ about the many affairs of his daily life. The experience of the saints has demonstrated that an amazing change occurs in one's life when he forms the daily habit of intimate, heart-to-heart conversation with Christ.

The Church, therefore, in its laws wisely obliges its priests "to spend some time each day in meditation." [7] Without it, the priest would lose intimate contact with Christ. This is not, of course, to deprecate vocal prayer; vocal prayer and meditation go hand-in-hand. But the priest (as well as the layman) experiences that a well made meditation enhances and enlivens his vocal prayer. In fact, it gives a new impetus to his entire spiritual life.

Meditation serves a twofold purpose in the spiritual life: it aids the soul to attain closer union with Christ, and it prevents our relapse into sin. The first is easily

---

[6] St. Teresa, *Way of Perfection*, xxi.

[7] Canon 125, 2. ". . . quotidie orationi mentali per aliquod tempus incumbant."

understood: our daily contact with Christ soon brings us into close union with Him. However, not many are aware of the fact that an absence of meditation places the soul in a perilous state of existence. St. Teresa reminds us: "Prayer is a necessity to prevent us from constantly falling into temptation." [8] Her co-worker in the reform of Carmel, St. John of the Cross, adds: "Without the aid of mental prayer, the soul cannot triumph over the forces of the demon." [9]

St. Teresa, writing of the lukewarm period of her life, confesses:

> I wish that I could obtain leave to declare the many times I failed during this period in my obligation to God, because I was not supported by the strong pillar of mental prayer.[10]

She informs us that she continued perseveringly, though poorly, in the practice of meditation; and this basic perseverance kept her at a minimum from mortal sin. Though she fell into venial sin and was harassed by temptations and trials, she was able to restrain from offending God seriously because of her practice of meditation. When St. Teresa finally succeeded in making her prayer not only with perseverance, but with fervor as well, she made rapid strides on the path of perfection. Little wonder that she could later claim:

> I am certain of it that Our Lord will eventually bring to the harbor of salvation, he who gives himself to prayer.[11]

---

[8] St. Teresa, *Interior Castle*, II, xx.

[9] St. John of the Cross, *Maxims*, n. 203.

[10] St. Teresa, *Life*, viii.

[11] *Ibid.* St. Alphonsus also offers a striking statement in the same vein: "And by experience we see that many persons who recite a great number of vocal prayers, the Office and the Rosary, fall into sin, and

Meditation, then, effects a complete change in a person's life, and adds a new tone to all his activities. The author recalls a conversation some years ago with a woman who had undertaken in earnest the practice of mental prayer. This devout lady, previously much occupied with the "things of the day," confided: "Those things which formerly interested me just don't seem to matter much anymore." Our Lord had given her a taste of His intimate friendship, and all else seemed insipid.

St. Teresa tells us that her own father was accustomed to visiting her convent quite frequently to chat lightly about the daily events in Avila. Then, St. Teresa initiated him in the science of meditation; and, to her amazement, her father did not visit the convent quite as frequently—he found too much to occupy him in meditation. And this is consonant with St. Teresa's doctrine of meditation: she states that those who practice meditation will receive from God consolation and "the joy of prayer." [12]

Meditation, naturally, consumes time. But this is not time lost; rather, the time expended in meditation aids in the ultimate conservation of time. This is true, first of all, because it places the soul under the direct influence of Christ, Who will then take complete charge of a person's activities. And, further, the added per-

---

continue to live in sin. But he who attends to mental prayer scarcely ever falls into sin, and should he have the misfortune of falling into it, he will hardly continue to live in so miserable a state; he will either give up mental prayer, or renounce sin. Meditation and sin cannot stand together. However abandoned a soul may be, if she perseveres in meditation, God will bring her to salvation." *Dignities and Duties of the Priest* (Brooklyn: Redemptorist Fathers, 1927), p. 292.

[12] St. Teresa, *Life*, viii.

spective gained in meditation will enable one to better regulate his life by the separation of the non-essential from the essential. Dom Chautard, in his magnificent book, *Soul of the Apostolate,* relates this enlightening incident:

> One of our great bishops, overburdened with his duties, explained this to a statesman, who also had too much to do. The latter had asked the bishop the secret of his constant work. "My dear friend," said the bishop, "add to your other occupations half an hour's meditation every morning. Not only will you get through your business, but you will find time for still more." [13]

Finally, St. Peter of Alcantara sums up for us the benefits of meditation in a vibrant passage:

> In mental prayer the soul is purified from its sins, nourished with charity, confirmed in faith, and strengthened in hope; the mind expands, the affections dilate, the heart is purified, truth becomes evident; temptation is conquered, sadness dispelled; the senses are renovated; drooping powers revive; tepidity ceases; the rust of vices disappears. Out of mental prayer issues forth, like living sparks, those desires of heaven which the soul conceives when inflamed with the fire of divine love. Sublime is the excellence of mental prayer, great are its privileges; to mental prayer heaven is opened; to mental prayer heavenly secrets are manifested and the ear of God ever attentive.[14]

In these days of whirlwind activity and deafening noise, it becomes more and more necessary to pause daily for interior conversation with Christ. Without this

---

[13] Dom Jean-Baptiste Chautard, *The Soul of the Apostolate* (Gethsemani: Trappist Fathers, 1946).

[14] St. Peter of Alcantara, *Treatise on Prayer,* 1st part.

daily period of meditation, the entire spiritual life stands in danger. Is this perhaps the reason that our Blessed Mother in her program of reparation inaugurated at Fatima has requested fifteen minutes *meditation* every first Saturday? At any rate, Pope Pius XII assures us that "no other means has the unique efficacy of meditation, and that as a consequence its daily practice can in no wise be substituted for."

3

SAINT TERESA'S CONCEPT
OF MEDITATION

WE HAVE EMPHASIZED, with calculated repetition, St. Teresa's fundamental theory of meditation: a loving conversation with Christ. St. Teresa, though, was a clever pedagogue; she realized that it is alarmingly difficult to kneel down and inaugurate conversation with Christ immediately. Human nature being what it is, our thoughts quickly wander from prayer. Therefore, she proposed a systematic approach to this conversation with Christ.

St. Teresa well understood the psychological mechanism of our human nature, and continually gives evidence of this knowledge in her writings. There are two principal interior faculties of man, intellect and will—or as they are termed in popular writing, mind and heart. The intellect (or mind) concerns itself with acts of reasoning, thought, and consideration; the will (or heart) is occupied with acts of a volitional nature, such as love and affection. It is through the intellect that one comes to the knowledge of some object, and through the will that he begins to love it. In other words, the intellect supplies the object for the will to love; and, correspondingly, nothing is loved by the will unless it has first been presented by the intellect.

Although meditation is principally centered in the will, St. Teresa is insistent that *both* intellect and will be employed if meditation is to prove successful. *In her program, she would have the intellect supply material for the conversation with Christ.* For example, the intellect is employed to consider the passion of Christ and His sufferings; and then the will is brought into play to talk with Christ about it, express its sorrow, or promise to avoid sin in the future.[1] In her plan, the meditation itself (or the consideration as we here term it) is the task of the intellect, while the conversation is the function of the will. The consideration is only a reasoning process by which the intellect turns the will towards Christ.

St. Teresa is careful to advise us against rushing into conversation with Christ until we are convinced we can sustain it. She admonishes us to picture Our Lord and think of Him in one of His mysteries, and then, when the heart is moved, speak to Him about the subject of the day's meditation. This procedure will result in an orderly plan for our conversation, and will hinder wan-

---

[1] The explanation of the workings of the intellect and the will in our treatise is presented in a popular manner. The author requests that the reader not restrict him to technical terminology. We are interested here in a psychological, rather than an ontological, description of the interior mechanism of human nature.

derings of the mind. The average individual is definitely not accustomed to this interior conversation, and, hence, St. Teresa would have him approach the problem systematically.

In her outline of prayer, St. Teresa clearly distinguishes the work of the intellect and the work of the will. To the intellectual process she adds a function known in psychology as the intellectual memory. In her treatment of the matter, the intellectual procedure embraces two elements: the formation of images from the memory, and intellectual reasoning. The intellectual memory depicts some scene in Christ's life, and the intellect itself examines it; then the will employs the result. Her concept of meditation might be depicted thus:

	Work of Intellect		*Work of Will*
Meditation =	Memory + Consideration	producing →	CONVERSATION WITH CHRIST

Needless to note, the conversation is the all-important element here; the work of the intellect merely prepares for the conversation and serves as a guide for it. Some souls require a greater amount of reasoning before they are able to begin their conversation; some require less. There is no hard and fast rule on the matter; here, as elsewhere, star differs from star.

This intellectual prelude to our conversation with Christ has frightened many. There is a general misunderstanding that meditation must be a process of reasoning, deductions, and syllogisms. Naturally, such a caricature of meditation is unappealing to most of us. Actually, there is nothing complicated or highly intellectual about it. In the consideration, St. Teresa merely asks us to carefully consider Christ in one of His mysteries in much the same manner as we examine a newspaper story about some figure in daily life.

In our prayer we are not to engage in subtle philosophic thought; nor are we to ponder over the truths of faith as would a speculative theologian. All St. Teresa would have us do is fill our minds and memories with Christ, so that we might more easily talk to Him. She wisely enunciates a fundamental rule of meditation: *that prayer consists not in thinking much, but in loving much.* But let us hear the saint herself on the matter:

> The first thing I wish to discuss, as far as my limited understanding will allow, is the nature of the essence of perfect prayer. For I have come across some people who believe that the whole thing consists in thought; and thus, if they are able to think a great deal about God, however much the effort may cost them, they immediately imagine they are spiritually minded; while, if they become distracted, and their efforts to think of good things fail, they at once become greatly discouraged and suppose themselves to be lost. I do not mean that it is not a favor from the Lord if any of us is able to continually meditate upon His works; and it is good for us to try to do this. But it must be recognized that not everyone has by nature an imagination capable of meditating, whereas all souls are capable of love. I have written elsewhere of what I believe to be the reasons for this wandering of the imagination . . . and so I am not discussing that now; I am only anxious to explain that the soul is not thought, nor is the will controlled by thought—it would be a great

misfortune if it were. The soul's profit, then, consists not in thinking much, but in loving much.[2]

Yet do not imagine I want you to make long meditations on our divine Saviour or much reasoning or profound and subtle conceptions. If you cannot do more, keep your eyes fixed for some moments on your adorable spouse.[3]

Those who reason much in prayer and find in any subject abundance of thoughts and considerations would do well to attend to the advice I am about to give. I would tell them not to give all the time of prayer to profoundly investigating the subject on which they are meditating. They will perhaps consider as lost the time thus not employed, but I consider it, on the contrary, a most precious gain. What then ought they to do? Let them place themselves in the presence of Our Lord and converse with Him, heart to heart, without fatiguing the understanding, and tasting the happiness of being in His company.[4]

The doctrine of St. Teresa should be clear: prayer does not consist in involved, complicated reasoning, but in thought which is productive of conversation with Christ.

This is St. Teresa's doctrine. But let us now listen to her as she gives an actual demonstration of true meditation:

We begin to meditate upon a scene of the Passion—let us say upon the binding of the Lord to the column. The mind sets to work to seek out the reasons which are to be found

---

[2] St. Teresa, *Book of Foundations*, v. Note that St. Teresa uses the term "meditation" in the more restricted sense—a division of the whole exercise known as "mental prayer." In our discussion, we have employed the term "consideration" for this part of prayer.

[3] St. Teresa, *Life*, xiii.

[4] *Ibid.*

for the great afflictions and distress which His Majesty must
have suffered when He was alone there. It also meditates on
the many other lessons which, if it is industrious, or well
stored with learning, this mystery can teach. This method
should be the beginning, the middle, and the end of prayer
for us: it is a most excellent and safe road until the Lord
leads us to other methods, which are supernatural . . . it is
well to reflect for a time and to think of the pains which He
bore there, why He bore them, Who He is that bore them
and with what love He suffered them. But we must not
always tire ourselves by going in search of such ideas; we
must sometimes remain by His side with our minds hushed
in silence. If we can, we should occupy ourselves in looking
upon Him Who is looking at us; keep Him company; talk
with Him; pray to Him; humble ourselves before Him; have
our delight in Him; and remember that He never deserved
to be there. Anyone who can do this, though he may be but
a beginner in prayer, will derive great benefit from it, for
this kind of prayer brings many benefits; at least, so my soul
has found.[5]

As we read St. Teresa's writings on meditation, we
are heartened by her understanding of human nature;
she is an accomplished psychologist. Her insistence
upon the employment of the intellect and memory during prayer is based on profound psychological truths.
She demands that our mind and our memory be sat-
urated with the thought of Christ before we commence
our conversation with Him. If we employ only our will,
leaving the mind and memory free, then our conversation will soon falter and distracting thoughts and memories will crowd out our prayer. Hence, it is necessary
to fill the mind and memory with Christ so that the

---

[5] *Ibid.*

entire organism—mind, memory, *and* heart—may be centered on Him.[6]

St. Teresa presents us a crystal-clear picture of meditation: the mind furnishing matter for the heart's talk with Christ. And, above all, her fundamental rule that *prayer consists not in thought, but in love.*

---

[6] It is not our intention to adopt the Augustinian theory of three principal interior faculties: memory, intellect, and will. We completely espouse St. Thomas' doctrine of the two interior faculties, intellect and will; and posit intellectual memory as a function of the intellect. However, for clarity's sake, we have made individual mention of the three functions here.

CHAPTER

4

A SIMPLIFIED METHOD
OF MEDITATION

DURING HER DAILY PERIOD of meditation St. Teresa
operated in an orderly manner; her prayer was not
a haphazard, rambling affair. We noted in the previous
chapter that she began her meditation with a consideration and remembrance of Christ in one of His mysteries, and progressed systematically to her conversation
with Him. In other words, St. Teresa followed a method
of prayer.

True, St. Teresa's method is quite different from the
involved procedures proposed to us by modern writers;
but it is definitely a method. Her method, or manner
of procedure, if you will, simply follows the workings
of our interior mechanism: intellect and memory result-
ing in acts of the will. Her method is not complicated:
it is, however, complete and sufficient.

It was not St. Teresa's intention to bind the soul to
a hard and fast method of prayer. She intends merely

to distinguish clearly the necessary elements preparatory to our conversation with Christ. If her outline is followed, it may be worked out in any framework of the individual's choosing.

But we think it essential that the beginner follow some logical procedure at meditation; else there is great danger of aimless mental wandering during the period of prayer. The employment of a method serves as a guide for the beginner; it is a lifesaver in times of dryness and aridity; and when distractions weary the soul, one can fall back upon the method immediately.

We find much prejudice levied against the employment of a method; and some of it is based on sound reasons. We do need a method; but we do not require an involved, intellectual "work out." There are two extremes to be avoided: overcomplexity, and lack of any method. The solution lies in between: the method of St. Teresa.

The method spells out the steps of meditation in a clear and logical order. As the soul progresses in prayer, these steps will be employed automatically without advertence to their application. It will be only in periods of dryness that one will find himself obliged to force through the method again to insure success at prayer.

Some will find that they need only spend a short period on the preliminaries, and can launch almost immediately into the conversation. Others will be obliged to expend much effort on the presence of God and consideration; and then find themselves able to stimulate but a short conversation with Christ. But *all* will be obliged to follow the steps of the method in some manner or other.

In outlining St. Teresa's method, we have attempted to arrange it in as simple a manner as possible. A brief reading of the schema should serve to impress it on the mind. The individual may then employ it at prayer without the necessity of reference to a meditation chart. On various occasions one will find that he may omit some of the steps. For example, one might approach his period of meditation well rooted in the presence of God. As in all other phases of life, common sense should be the guiding factor.

We have outlined five general steps in St. Teresa's method of meditation:

1. *Preparation:* It is difficult to launch into prayer from the midst of a flurry of distracting occupations. Almost all of us are forced to pause momentarily and place ourselves before Our Lord in the Blessed Sacrament, or God as He resides in the soul. A good beginning is half the battle.

2. *Selection of the Material:* Having reminded oneself of Christ's presence, one is next obliged to select a subject for the day's conversation. This is ordinarily best done by reading from some book suited for meditation, preferably the Gospels. Or it may be accomplished by the study of a picture or statue of Our Lord.

3. *The Consideration:* After Christ's presence has been recalled and the proper material selected, the individual begins the examination of the day's matter. In this study of the material, one asks himself the tra-

ditional questions: Who is here in this scene? What is He doing? Why is He doing it? What does it mean to me?

4. *The Conversation:* Now one is prepared to undertake the principal part of meditation, that for which all the preceding steps have been devised. The soul begins to talk slowly to Christ, telling Him of its love for Him, its desire to serve Him, its willingness to do anything for Him. He adores Christ in the scene of the day's meditation; he expresses his love for Him; thanks Him for past gifts; petitions Him for new favors in the future. When the conversation begins to falter, it will be necessary to return briefly to the consideration to stimulate new thoughts for additional conversation with Christ.

5. *The Conclusion:* This is an entirely optional step; but we feel it to be of great value in making progress in prayer. Near the close of the meditation period, it would be well for one to tie up the loose ends. Our Lord should be thanked for the graces received during the time of prayer now coming to a conclusion. Then, very briefly, one might examine his failings during the period, and promise to eradicate these in the future. This determination to hold better conversation with Christ in succeeding periods gives one a strong determination to make further strides along the road of prayer. And with this burst of enthusiasm and promise for the future, the day's prayer is concluded.

This method is contractible; it can be used for a five-minute or an hour's meditation. Of course, in the longer meditation, it will be necessary to repeat steps three and four a number of times during the period. But one of its major advantages is that it can be employed during a short visit to the Blessed Sacrament, or in a long, formal period of meditation. It is entirely pliable.

We cannot emphasize too strongly the necessity of following some such outline, especially as one first undertakes the practice of meditation. The modern, twentieth-century man is completely unaccustomed to the rarefied air of the interior life, and will certainly wander and stumble if he does not possess an outline to follow. If one begins prayer with this methodical procedure, he can be sure to make progress. St. Teresa is insistent that we attack this problem with a grim determination. And one of the best evidences of good faith in the matter is to proceed systematically to one's conversation with Christ.

OUTLINE OF MEDITATION

General purpose: to hold loving conversation with Christ.

1. *Preparation:*
   Place oneself in the presence of Christ.

2. *Selection of the material:*
   Read; or study a picture of Christ.

3. *Consideration:*
   Reflect upon the material. Ask oneself the questions: who, what, why, for what reason?

4. *Conversation:* (Core of the Meditation)

> *Converse with Our Lord about the material. Employ the affections of love, adoration, thanksgiving, sorrow, petition.*

5. *Conclusion:*

> Gratitude to Christ for favors received. Examination of faults during meditation, and resolution of further effort in succeeding meditations.

II

Explanation of the Method

"What great blessings God grants to a soul when He prepares it to love the practice of prayer."

—St. Teresa

CHAPTER

5

GENERAL PREPARATION
FOR MEDITATION

THE BEST OVER-ALL preparation for successful meditation is a personal conviction of its importance and
a staunch determination to persevere in its practice. If
one has acquired this attitude of mind, he has made a
splendid preparation for his meditation.

St. Teresa gives us this important admonition:

> It is essential, I maintain, to begin the practice of prayer
> with a firm resolution to persevere in it.[1]

If one be not convinced of the necessity of meditation in his own life, nor resolved never to omit its daily
exercise, he will soon give it up on one pretext or another. Therefore, one should not adopt the practice of
meditation with the intention of "giving it a try"; but
rather, one must undertake the exercise with a firm
belief that it is of the utmost importance that he begin
and persevere in it. Our mental attitude towards any

---

[1] St. Teresa, *Way of Perfection*, xxi.

enterprise will determine, to a large extent, our success in it; meditation is no exception.

Meditation, furthermore, is not an isolated experience in one's spiritual life. For, as St. Augustine maintains, the science of prayer is the science of life. To engage in a satisfactory conversation with Christ during a given fifteen-minute period, it is necessary to employ other spiritual aids throughout the *entire day*. Chief among these are: recollection, spiritual reading, mortification, and the cultivation of a humble heart. These will all be discussed more fully in Part VI; it will suffice to comment briefly upon them here.

It is, understandably, much easier to unite ourselves with Christ during a meditation period if we have remained in contact with Him throughout the day in the midst of our duties and occupations. This happy state can be effected by an exercise known in spiritual terminology as "the presence of God." It consists basically in evoking aspirations and short prayers to Our Lord at various intervals during the day. The employment of such an exercise is of incalculable help in one's prayer life. Daily spiritual reading will furnish thoughts, ideas, and background for our conversation with Christ. The more we know about Our Lord, the more we will appreciate Him and be able to speak intelligently to Him. Then, too, a generous program of mortification aids greatly in perfecting one's meditation. Mortification serves a twofold purpose: it detaches one from loves and attachments which hinder the soul's affection for Christ; and it gives one the self-mastery and discipline so necessary during meditation. Finally, the cultivation of a humble heart assures us of avoiding an excessive preoccupation with ourselves during the period of meditation. We will find our sufficiency in Christ and tend to depend on Him rather than upon ourselves.

All of these measures will make for better meditation. Above all, though, one's attitude to the practice is of primary importance. If a proper attitude be lacking, then one's hope of success is almost nil. To insure perseverance in meditation, therefore, one should determine the precise time at which he will meditate each day. And only on rare occasions and for most pressing reasons should he ever omit his meditation at that time. If one has not selected a definite hour for his prayer, he will discover more often than not he will omit it. Some find it easier to meditate in the morning, others in the evening. Each one should choose the time most suited for him in relation to his temperament and occupations. But, whether he select morning or evening (or better yet, both), he should choose some definite time at which he will meet Christ for his daily conversation with Him.

Cardinal Mercier relates this penetrating bit of insight on the matter:

> It would appear that before the close of the Middle Ages the masters of the spiritual life did not deem it needful to appoint a fixed hour each day for meditation. At the present day, however, this custom is not only advisable, it is absolutely necessary. Such is the hurry and bustle of modern life, such the multiplicity of interests and of social obligations, that it has become almost impossible for men to lead a life of union with God unless they reserve one tranquil hour for Him in the early morning, before the whirlwind of their

occupations carries them off, covering their souls with its blinding dust and deafening them with its noise.[2]

One must also convince himself that his efforts will eventually be rewarded with success, that he will learn to make satisfactory conversation with Our Lord. The hope of success—and success is here assured—is always an enticement to persevering effort. St. Teresa offers us this consolation:

> Besides the courage we ought to have in the combat of mental prayer, we must also be firmly convinced that, unless we allow' ourselves to be vanquished, our efforts will be crowned with success.[3]

Hence, the determined soul need never give way to feelings of discouragement. Despite the difficulties entailed and the persevering effort required, ultimate victory will be ours. The only disaster is to cease trying.

These, therefore, are the attitudes we should bring to prayer. They will insure that we launch into prayer with determination and perseverance—and with confidence in our ultimate success.

---

[2] Cardinal Mercier, *Conferences*, trans. by J. M. O'Kavanagh (Westminster: Newman, 1943), p. 104.

[3] St. Teresa, *Way of Perfection*, xxiii.

CHAPTER

6

IMMEDIATE PREPARATION
FOR MEDITATION

THE TIME of meditation is at hand! A suitable hour
has been selected, and the person kneels to begin
his conversation with Christ. First of all, the presence
of Our Lord is recalled to mind. If meditation is made
before the Blessed Sacrament, this is readily accomplished. A glance at the Tabernacle, with a consideration of Our Lord's abiding presence in the Host, will
serve to center one's attention on Christ. But even
when the meditation is undertaken apart from the
Blessed Sacrament, it should be relatively easy to consider the penetrating presence of Christ, Who is always
near to each of us and ready to hear our every prayer.[1]

---

[1] The presence of Christ's Humanity is, naturally, confined to His
existence in heaven and in the tabernacles of the world. Yet, His
Humanity looks on us from afar, and is accordingly present to us.
Furthermore, we possess the Three Persons of the Blessed Trinity in
our soul through Divine Grace. And the Second Person, while present
only in His Divinity, nevertheless has an habitual relation to His
Humanity; and in this manner, Christ might be said to have presence
in our souls.

But wherever the meditation be made, the important factor is the development of a conscious realization that Christ is close to us and willing to engage in conversation with us. For most of us, engulfed as we are in a flurry of distracting occupations, this momentary pause to consider Christ's nearness is essential.

Having noted the necessity of drawing close to Our Lord, we are confronted with two incidental questions: what posture should we assume at prayer; how should we regulate our eyes during the period? A word about each will suffice.

St. Teresa advises us to choose a comfortable position at prayer; but, she wisely adds, a position that is not too comfortable—else drowsiness might set in. Meditation is a period in which we unite ourselves with God; it should not be devoted to the practice of physical mortifications entailed in rigid posture, or the like. It might be better to begin our meditation on our knees. This will aid us in drawing our attention to Christ; but when bodily weariness begins to assert itself, it is entirely proper to change one's position. Hence, prayer may be made while sitting, or standing, or even while walking. Here again the individual must select for himself the posture most conducive to his own meditation.

Apropos of this, there is the story of the old farmer who, when interrogated as to his opinion of the most desirable posture for prayer, retorted: "Well, I don't know. I was leaning over the edge of the well last week when I slipped and went flying down the well head first. I'll tell you, I said the best prayers of my life while dropping down that well standing on my head." Therefore, any posture can be conducive to good meditation. Or, as St. Teresa counsels, a comfortable position that is not too comfortable.

As regards the position of the eyes, common sense should furnish the answer. We definitely will not be able to sustain a conversation with Christ while we are gazing at passersby, or studying the interior of some church.[2] If we make our meditation in a place free from noise or commotion, it might be possible to keep our eyes open and continue our conversation with Christ. But if one is in the midst of a variety of distractions, the eyes must, of necessity, remain closed. As a general rule, St. Teresa encourages us to keep our eyes constantly shut during prayer. She notes that this will be extremely difficult at first; but after a short while, one will find himself unable to meditate unless his eyes are closed.[3]

At the beginning of prayer, St. Teresa advises the soul to humble itself before God. This can be done by

[2] St. Teresa offers some pertinent advice on this matter: "The first lesson which Our Lord gives us to pray well is, you know, to retire into solitude, as He always did Himself; not that He had any need of this solitude, but for our instruction, and to give us an example. One cannot speak to God and at the same time to the world; yet this is what they do, who, while praying on the one side, listen on the other to what is said near them, or stop at everything which comes into their mind, without trying to withdraw their attention from it." *Way of Perfection*, xxv.

[3] Her exact statement: "Those who practice recollection, when they are in prayer, nearly always have their eyes closed; and it is an excellent custom for many reasons, because it is doing oneself violence in order to turn one's eyes away from the things of the earth. However, it is only in the beginning that it costs; in fact, when one has acquired the habit thereof, it rather requires violence to open the eyes than to close them." *Ibid.*, xxvii.

a brief consideration of one's own faults. The rather frightening example of the pharisee and the publican comes to mind—"O God, be merciful to me the sinner . . . this man went back to his home justified rather than the other." [4] We must not open our conversation with God while we are preoccupied with our own self-importance—this defect can be combatted by the realization of our faults and a humble admission of them.

St. Teresa, in her treatise on prayer, *The Way of Perfection*, outlines for us the early moments of meditation—humble admission of one's weakness and a keen realization of Christ's presence:

> As you know, the first thing must be examination of conscienc confession of sin and the signing of yourself with the Cross. Then, daughter, as you are alone, you must look for a companion—and who could be a better companion than the very Master who taught you the prayer that you are about to say? Imagine that this Lord Himself is at your side and see how lovingly and how humbly He is teaching you—and, believe me, you should stay with so good a friend as long as you can before you leave Him. If you become accustomed to having Him at your side, and if He sees that you love Him to be there, and are always trying to please Him, you will never be able, as we put it, to send Him away, nor will He ever fail you. . . . Do you think it is a small thing to have such a friend as that beside you? [5]

It is of paramount importance, therefore, that at the beginning of our meditation we place ourselves squarely in the presence of Christ, our friend, who is calling us to a heart-to-heart conversation.

---

[4] Luke, 18, 14.
[5] St. Teresa, *ibid.*, xxvi.

CHAPTER

7

SELECTION OF THE
MATERIAL

THE NEARNESS of Christ has now been assessed.
There next arises the problem of selecting suitable
material for the day's meditation. Before further progress can be made, one must choose carefully the subject
matter of his conversation with Christ. In this area, the
soul is definitely given wide latitude, but some basic
rules may be offered as a guide.

It sometimes happens—although not with frequent
occurrence in the case of beginners—that the soul begins the period of prayer well supplied with material
for the day's conversation. The death of a loved one,
for instance, may so engage one's attention that it will
serve as an excellent entree to conversation with Christ,
the consoler of hearts. Or some aspect of Christ's life
may have occupied one for a period outside the time of
meditation, so that he is able to turn to it quite readily
during prayer. Then, too, as one becomes more pro-

ficient in the spiritual life and acquires a habitual attitude of recollection, the need of preparation becomes
less and less necessary until it is almost nonexistent. But
most often, especially in the initial stages of friendship
with Christ, it will be necessary to make a positive selection of material for the meditation period.

This selection is more readily accomplished by reading from some book which is in itself provocative of
conversation with Christ. The most serviceable book in
this regard, of course, would be *The New Testament.*
In it, one finds depicted the personality of Christ, and
from its pages there stands out in bold relief the true
picture of our Divine Friend. It is well to remember
that, while one may meditate on any subject—the final
destiny of man, our sins in the sight of God, the virtues
to be practiced—he should devote the major part of his
meditations to Christ, the God-man. St. Teresa is quite
insistent that in our prayer life, we regularly center our
attention upon the Humanity of Christ. She maintains
that even those in the higher stages of the spiritual life
must retain contact with the Humanity of Our Lord.
Writing of this in her *Interior Castle,* she contends:

> . . . however spiritual you are, you must not flee so com-
> pletely from corporeal things as to think that meditation on
> the most Sacred Humanity can actually harm you.
>
> Some souls imagine that they cannot dwell upon the Pas-
> sion, in which case they will be able still less to meditate
> upon the most sacred Virgin and the lives of the saints, the
> remembrance of which brings us such great profit and en-
> couragement. I cannot conceive what they are thinking of.
> . . . We need to cultivate, and think upon and seek the com-
> panionship of those who, though living on earth like our-

selves, have accomplished such great deeds for God; the last thing we should do is to withdraw of set purpose from our greatest help and blessing, which is the most Sacred Humanity of Our Lord Jesus Christ.[1]

St. Teresa is in perfect accord with the traditional doctrine of the Church: the last thing we should ever consider in our prayer life is the omission of our contact with Christ. Hence, our meditation period will find us frequently occupied with Our Lord, His life, and His doctrine.

A saint of our own times, St. Therese of Lisieux, has commented on her frequent use of the Gospels during her meditation periods:

> . . . during meditation I am sustained above all else by the Gospels. They supply my poor soul's every need, and they are always yielding up to me new lights and mysterious hidden meanings. I know from experience that 'the kingdom of God is within us,' that Jesus has no need of books or doctors to instruct our soul; He, the Doctor of Doctors, teaches us without the sound of words.[2]

Our prayer need not be exclusively Christo-centric. We may, and should include other subjects in our meditations, but the life of Christ will be a frequently recurring theme. St. Teresa expresses the proper approach in her autobiography:

> . . . There will be many souls who derive greater benefits from other meditations than from that of the Sacred Passion. For, just as there are many mansions in heaven, so there are

---

[1] St. Teresa, *Interior Castle*, vii.

[2] St. Therese of Lisieux, *The Story of a Soul*, trans. by Michael Day (Westminster: Newman, 1952), p. 129.

many roads to them. Some people derive benefit from imagining themselves in hell; others, whom it distresses to think
of hell, from imagining themselves in heaven. Others meditate on death. Some, who are tenderhearted, get exhausted
if they keep thinking about the Passion, but they derive
great comfort and benefit from considering the power and
greatness of God in the creatures, and the love that He
showed us, which is pictured in all things. This is an ad-
mirable procedure, provided one does not fail to meditate
often upon the Passion and the life of Christ, which are, and
have always been, the source of everything that is good.[3]

It was noted above that the selection of the material
is most readily accomplished through the use of a book.
Hence, this phase of the meditation has come to be
known as the "reading." A book is read for a few minutes—perhaps five or ten minutes, or only two or three,
if that be sufficient. This reading, performed immediately prior to meditation, is an exercise distinct from the
daily spiritual reading. Spiritual reading, as envisioned
in the minds of the saints and spiritual experts, ought
to occupy one for at least fifteen minutes each day. Its
purpose is to instruct in the spiritual life, to give principles and axioms for daily living, to demonstrate sanc-
tity as it is practised in the lives of the saints. The
meditative reading before prayer, on the other hand,
has as its aim the presentation of material for meditation.[4]

---

[3] St. Teresa, *Life*, xiii.
[4] Dom Chautard, *op. cit.*, p. 199, notes: "A book of meditations is
almost necessary to keep the mind from drifting around in a fog.
There are plenty of works, old and new, that have everything that is
demanded in a true book of meditations, as distinct from spiritual
reading. Each point contains some striking truth presented in a clear,

The amount that one reads in this meditative reading is of no consequence. A few sentences or paragraphs may serve its purpose; or it may be found that the reading of a number of pages be necessary. This reading is to be performed slowly and attentively—and not with the rapidity customary in other forms of reading. When one has focused his attention on the subject matter of the reading and obtained sufficient material for meditation, he may then put the book aside. It has served its purpose.

If, for instance, one is to meditate on the Passion of Our Lord, he might begin to read carefully the twenty-seventh chapter of St. Matthew's Gospel. As he reads, he becomes impressed with the fierce punishments inflicted upon Christ, and his attention becomes riveted upon the suffering Jesus. The material for the day's meditation is thus selected and brought to the front of one's consciousness. From this point, one continues to reflect on the scene, and eventually concludes in a conversation with Christ about His Passion.

Although the book should be relinquished after a short period of careful reading, it is not to be concluded that it may not be employed again during the period of prayer. Quite to the contrary. After one has reflected on the subject of the meditation and spoken to Christ about it, the affections and attention begin to lag. It then becomes necessary to begin again; and so the book

---

forceful, and concise manner, in such a way that once we have reflected upon it, we are inevitably led on into a loving and practical conversation with God."

is reopened to start off on a new subject, or to continue the previous one.

St. Teresa, one of the Church's foremost contemplatives, was often found at prayer with a book in her hand. Writing of one period of her life, she states:

> During all these years, except after communicating, I never dared begin to pray without a book; my soul was as much afraid to engage in prayer without one as if it were to go and fight against a host of enemies. With this help, which was a companionship to me and a shield with which I could parry the blows of my many thoughts, I felt comforted. For it was not usual with me to suffer from aridity: this only came when I had no book, whereupon my soul would at once become disturbed and my thoughts begin to wander. As soon as I started to read they began to collect themselves and the book acted like a bait to my soul. Often the mere fact that I had it by me was sufficient. Sometimes I read a little, sometimes a great deal, according to the favor which the Lord showed me.[5]

That which is accomplished through the employment of a book may also be effected by use of a picture. Before meditation one might gaze on a picture of one of the scenes of Our Lord's life, and the scene contemplated would serve as the subject of the meditation. St. Teresa also mentions this practice in her treatise on prayer:

> You will find it very helpful if you can get an image or a picture of this Lord—one that you like—not to wear round your neck and never look at, but to use regularly whenever you talk to Him, and He will tell you what to say.[6]

---

[5] St. Teresa, *Life*, iv.
[6] St. Teresa, *Way of Perfection*, xxvi.

If a book is used, it should be carefully selected. Besides collections of meditations, books which explain the many manifestations of God's love for us may be profitably employed. It is well, however, to make use of standard works that are better known. Ultimately, though, the choice of reading depends upon the educational background and the spiritual development of the individual. Books that are either intellectually or spiritually too advanced will cause dryness in prayer and, accordingly, defeat their very purpose. One might look for suitable material in some of these works: *The New Testament,*[7] *Imitation of Christ,* writings of St. Francis de Sales, St. Alphonsus Liguori, St. Teresa of Avila, St. Therese of Lisieux.

This particular step of the procedure, therefore, has as its purpose the selection of the material for the day's meditation. Through the use of a book or picture—if this still be necessary in the individual's spiritual life— one centers his attention on the matter which is to serve as the subject of his conversation with Christ.

[7] The Confraternity of the Precious Blood has published a harmony of the four Gospels, *Christ in the Gospel* (Brooklyn: 1951), which presents a handsome line-drawing to illustrate each of the incidents of Christ's life. This pocket-size book, combining Gospel text and accompanying illustrations, makes an excellent volume for use during meditation.

CHAPTER

8

THE CONSIDERATION

THE STAGE for meditation has been set. There now remains but a single step before the satisfying conversation with Christ may be commenced—the mysterious and oft misunderstood *consideration*. The consideration (or *meditation*, as it is termed by many authors) has been misconstrued as the essential core of meditative prayer; while in reality, it should serve as a prelude to the real function of meditation.[1]

During the consideration period one applies his memory, imagination, and intellect to the subject matter selected for the day's prayer. This is done so as to provide suitable material for the ensuing conversation. The work of the intellect (to which is co-joined the memory and imagination) is entailed here; the will is brought into play during the succeeding step.

The memory works over the selected material in an attempt to recall previous knowledge about the subject,

---

[1] *Cf. supra,* p. 4, for a discussion of the convertible terms "meditation" and "consideration."

and bring it to the forefront of one's consciousness. Through the employment of the imagination, the subject matter is made vividly present to the mind. And, finally, the intellect thinks out the meditation material so as to arrive at an understanding of its meaning and of its relationship to the individual soul.

It might be beneficial to consider briefly the role of the imaginative faculty in this part of the meditation. The assistance of the imagination is enlisted to depict in one's mind a mystery or scene in Our Lord's life. This is done to facilitate the consequent reflection which will be dependent, to some extent, upon the representation of the imagination.[2]

There has been a good deal of discussion among spiritual writers as to the exact amount of imaginative detail to be employed at meditation. Some commentators demand that a detailed imaginative picture be worked out.[3] Others are wary of an over-stimulation of the imagination.[4] It is difficult to formulate a general prac-

---

[2] St. Francis de Sales (*Introduction to a Devout Life*, II, 4) gives his reader, Philothea, an exhortation upon the necessity of the imaginative faculty in meditation:

"By means of the imagination we confine our mind within the mystery on which we meditate, that it may not ramble to and fro, just as we shut up a bird in a cage, or tie a hawk by her leash, that she may rest on the hand. Some may perhaps tell you that it is better to use the simple thought of faith, mental and spiritual, in the representation of these mysteries, or else to imagine that the things take place in your own soul. But this method is too subtle for beginners; therefore, until it shall please God to raise you higher, I advise you, Philothea, to remain in the low valley which I have shown you."

[3] Especially St. Ignatius of Loyola and his "composition of place." (*Cf. The Spiritual Exercises*, 47, 91, 103, 112.)

[4] *Cf.* Father Gabriel of St. Mary Magdalen, O.C.D., *Little Catechism*

tical rule, for temperaments of individuals differ: some persons enjoy an amazing facility at imaginative conjecturing, and others find it difficult to arrive at any really satisfactory imaginative thought.

St. Teresa recognized the inherent value of imaginative representation in prayer—that it serves to center one's powers of attention on the meditation, and aids in warding off distractions. However, St. Teresa would have the tyro at meditation tread a middle path by striving for neither too much nor too little detail in imagination. All earnest effort should be applied in arriving at some useable imaginative representation; but definite limitations and restrictions must be established here. The imaginative faculty is to be enlisted only to serve as an introduction to prayer; it should not be employed beyond that goal. It is sometimes erroneously concluded that prayer has been successful when one has managed to develop vividly in his imagination some scene from Christ's life; but a satisfactory imaginative picture is not necessarily a guarantee of good prayer. Some souls may be quite adept in conjecturing an imaginative representation, and then engage in rather poor prayer. On the other hand, some may succeed in forming only a sketchy representation, and then proceed to an excellent period of prayer.

St. Teresa advises all to strive vigorously to capture some type of imaginative representation. But she does

---

of Prayer, trans. by Discalced Carmelite Nuns (Concord, 1949), p. 27. Father Gabriel notes some of the hazards attendant upon an overstimulation of the imagination; viz., the danger of provoking vivid representations which might be mistaken for visions and ecstasies.

concede that each one has different capabilities in this department. For those who are little adept at imagining she would offer the solace that a vague representation suffices at prayer. For those who enjoy a facility of imagination she extends the encouragement to utilize their gift in prayer. However, she would advise all to realize that imagination is not prayer; and, consequently, a limited time and effort should be expended upon it.

It might offer a bit of consolation to those who experience difficulty in imaginative thought—and we all do at some time or other—to know that St. Teresa herself had such difficulties. She writes of her problem:

My coarse understanding has never been able to picture the images of heavenly and sublime objects. . . . Others, by the help of a lively imagination, represent to themselves what they wish to meditate upon and thus they become recollected; with me, this faculty was so inert that it could not in any manner picture what I did not see with my eyes. There was only one thing in my power, and that was to think of Jesus Christ as man. But in vain books pictured to me His beauty; in vain were pictures of Him daily before my eyes; never was it possible for me to represent to myself interiorly the features of the God-man. Faith alone showed Him present to me. Imagine a blind man or somebody in the midst of profound darkness conversing with another person; he knows for certain and believes that this person is there, for he hears him, but he does not see him. Thus was it with me when I thought of Our Lord; I saw Him only with the eyes of faith.[5]

Finally, St. Teresa offers this advice which places imagination in its proper perspective in relation to the entire meditation:

---

[5] St. Teresa, *Life*, ix.

Not everyone has by nature an imagination capable of meditation; whereas all souls are capable of love.[6]

The mentai representation of the scene from Christ's life is perhaps most easily effected by imagining that the one meditating is actually present at the particular scene or event. This serves to place one in immediate contact with the meditation material. St. Teresa strongly advises this practice; and St. Francis de Sales describes it as *the* standard method of meditation:

> . . . there remains a third point which consists in representing to your imagination the whole of the mystery on which you desire to meditate, as if it really passed in your presence. For example, if you meditate on the crucifixion of Our Lord, imagine that you are on Mount Calvary, and that you there behold and hear all that was done or said at the time of Our Lord's passion. Or, if you prefer, imagine that they are crucifying Our Saviour in the very place in which you are, in the manner described by the holy evangelists.[7]

This personal introduction into the scene of the meditation has great value. It is an excellent device for the beginner to move quickly into the essential steps of meditation.

Let us suppose, to take St. Teresa's favorite subject of prayer, that we have elected to meditate upon the scene of Our Lord's scourging at the pillar. What are the precise steps to be taken in this part of meditation known as the consideration? . . . The reading of the Gospel narrative immediately prior to meditation has served to recall the basic facts of the event. One also

---

[6] St. Teresa, *Foundations*, v.
[7] St. Francis de Sales, *Loc. cit.*

calls to mind various snatches of former reading about Christ's scourging—the time, place, general manner of Roman punishments, etc. The imagination is then stimulated in the manner described above. An attempt is made to form a mental picture of the scourging without too intense an effort to reproduce all the details of the event—a vague, general picture suffices. One is advised, following the suggestion of St. Teresa and St. Francis de Sales, to introduce himself into the scene by imagining that he is actually standing next to the pillar at which Christ is receiving His flagellation.

At this point one begins the series of reflections intended to provoke the conversation with Our Lord. St. Teresa counsels us to consider: Who it is that suffers, what He suffers, how, why, and with what dispositions. These questions represent a survey of the classical "circumstances" employed by the scholastic philosophers to judge the importance and significance of any event or occurrence.[8] We employ the "circumstances", albeit unknowingly, almost daily in our lives to arrive at a full comprehension of some aspect of reality. For instance, in reading a newspaper account of an event we unconsciously seek out the answers to the "circumstances"— who, what, when, etc. St. Teresa simply asks us to apply the seven questions of the "circumstances" to our subject of meditation so as to come to a mature understanding of its true significance. The seven circum-

---

[8] The seven "circumstances" are known in scholastic philosophy as "circumstantae rationabiles." They are: quis, quid, ubi, quibus auxiliis, cur, quomodo, quando. (Who, what, where, with what assistance, why, how, when.) *Cf.* St. Thomas Aquinas, *Summa Theologica*, 1, 2, q. 7, a. 1.

stances (who, what, where, when, how, why, with what assistance) as applied in meditation aid us to proceed with the consideration in an orderly and rapid manner. But, while their assistance is extremely useful, it is not necessary to adhere rigidly to them. We may, with perfect freedom, allow our mind to investigate the subject from any angle, provided it will help stimulate the ensuing conversation.

As the result of these reflections, the soul will become aware of the love of Christ for it, the frightening tortures Christ endured to prove this love, and the horrendous nature of personal sin which has caused this suffering. These convictions, if sufficiently grasped, will almost automatically turn the soul to conversation with Christ. ✓

It would be a mistake, however, to terminate the reflections and inaugurate the conversation as soon as the initial pious affection has been experienced. The danger would be that this elusive affection might quickly vanish, leaving the soul barren and dry. The reflections and considerations should be continued until they make a definite impression on the consciousness of the individual. It is impossible to place an exact time limit upon the duration of the consideration, for many factors enter here: state of spiritual progress, intelligence, degree of attention, etc. As a general pattern, though, beginners at meditation will necessarily be compelled to spend more time on the consideration and less on the conversation following it. As the soul progresses, the ratio will slowly be inverted, so that a major part of the meditation will be consumed in conversation after a relatively brief consideration period.

But whatever be the needs or condition of the individual, one should not pass on to the conversation until the significance of the meditation material has been duly impressed upon him.

We can conceivably be frightened into assuming that this step entails an enervating intellectual drill; but this is far from the actual situation. We do not investigate the meditation material as would a student his text book. Rather, we reflect on the subject matter of meditation in much the same manner as one reads an important letter from a friend—carefully, lovingly, and with attention to its meaning. Our consideration is not to be a tense, analytic survey of some event of Christ's life; it is, on the contrary, a gentle, loving attempt to discover the significance of this episode of Our Lord's life as it relates to us.[9]

Listen to St. Teresa as she describes her method of reflecting upon Christ's scourging at the pillar:

> The mind sets to work to seek out the reasons which are to be found for the great afflictions and distress which His Majesty must have suffered when He was alone there . . . it is well to reflect for a time and to think of the pains which He

---

[9] It can readily be ascertained why this type of meditation has been labeled "discursive prayer." "Discourse" was the term employed by the ancient Latins to designate the method of thought through which one arrived at the truth gradually by a process of induction—one truth leading to a higher truth. Discursive prayer, consequently, is that form of prayer in which we work from point to point, or conclusion to conclusion, until the desired result has been achieved—in this case, a truth vivid and forceful enough to evoke conversation with Christ.

bore there, why He bore them, who He is that bore them and with what love He suffered them.[10]

Note that St. Teresa applies some of the "circumstances" to the meditation material. This is a highly advisable procedure; the mind tends to wander, and this artificial system of reflection aids in keeping it on its path. Naturally, not every one of the seven "circumstances" need be applied to each meditation subject— only as many as are felt to be necessary and useful.

This, then, is the nature and function of the step known as the *consideration*. There is nothing complicated about it; all that is required is that one approach it with an understanding of its purpose, and the intention of serious application. To recapitulate: one selects some scene from Christ's life; he imagines himself present at the particular scene; he investigates the scene by the use of the seven "circumstances." This should prove sufficient to project him into conversation with Christ.

[10] St. Teresa, *Life*, xiii.

CHAPTER

9

THE CONVERSATION—
HEART OF THE MEDITATION

A T LONG LAST the focal point of meditation—the conversation—has been reached. If the preceding
stages of meditation have been delineated at some
length, it was not to imply that an extended period of
time need necessarily be consumed upon them; these
steps may, in some cases, be completed with dispatch.

We presume that the person meditating has now examined the scene of Christ's life—and initiated himself
into it—so as to have at his disposal some subject matter
for his conversation. His reflections during the step
prior to the conversation should have supplied him with
a topic for the colloquy and some incentive to engage
in it. At this point in the procedure, the one meditating
begins to talk slowly, sincerely, and directly to Christ
about the significance and nature of the event (or mystery) upon which he has reflected. In the preceding
step, the scene was examined objectively in a consideration of Christ in the third person—He did this, He

55

suffered that; here Christ is approached in the second person—You did this, You suffered that. The soul talks to Christ easily and without strain, in much the same manner as we would address one of our close friends. The choice of words and manner in expression are in no wise of any importance; in fact, a studied attempt to phrase well-turned expressions might defeat the very purpose of meditation by placing an obstacle between Christ and the soul. We are to speak frankly and without affectation to Christ. Our Lord, amazingly enough, is exceedingly fond of each one of us, and wishes to meet us face-to-face; the struggle to offer studied thoughts and words to Christ hinders this intimate contact. The published prayers of saints and spiritual writers have a definite value in the spiritual life—they demonstrate a method and outline for conversation with Our Lord. But Christ would be sorely disappointed were we to hide behind the words of these prayers. Our Blessed Lord wishes us to talk to Him in our own words and with our own expressions, as awkward and as ungrammatical as they may be. When the moment for our conversation with Christ arrives, He is not the least interested in the prayers and sentiments of some saint or ascetic who lived hundreds of years ago; He wants to hear our words and our sentiments. Nothing more is required; nothing less would be satisfactory. St. Teresa comments on this:

> With regard to the habit of conversing often with your Divine Spouse, be confident that He will suggest to your heart what to say. You are not embarrassed when you speak to His creatures, why should words fail you when you wish to speak

to your God? Do not believe that will happen to you: for my part, at least, I look on that as impossible if you have acquired the habit of this interior conversation with Our Lord.[1]

The soul can picture itself in the presence of Christ, and accustom itself to becoming enkindled with great love for His sacred humanity and to have Him ever with it and speak with Him, ask Him for the things it has need of, make complaints to Him of its trials, rejoice with Him in its joys and yet never allow its joys to make it forgetful of Him. It has no need to think out set prayers but can use just such words as suit its desires and needs.[2] √

St. Teresa makes her point deftly: if we can talk to our acquaintances, why can we not talk to Christ? No one requires training in the art of conversation; it is a natural habit acquired early in life. Well enough, then! Let us apply our natural facility for conversation to this colloquy with Christ. Our Lord has expressed our relationship to Him in quite human terms—"I call you now not servants, but friends";[3] He expects us to fulfill our part of the relationship in the most common act of friendship, intimate conversation.

Our conversation with Christ need not be expressed vocally; indeed, this is to be discouraged. We may, if we so desire, form interior, non-expressed words as part of our conversation—in fact, it is highly advisable that beginners at meditation do just this. As one develops a greater facility for meditation, he will find himself capable of expression in non-verbal sentiments of the

---

[1] St. Teresa, *Way of Perfection*, xvii.
[2] St. Teresa, *Life*, xii.
[3] John, 17, 15.

heart and will: love, gratitude, sorrow, etc. Or again, this conversation with Our Lord may take the form of a simple enjoyment of Christ's presence with a few concomitant emotions of affection and esteem. The individual's psychological makeup and his stage of development at prayer will be the determining factor here as to the choice of procedures employed. √

Our conversation with Christ during the period of meditation is to be a continued, protracted discussion. It is not necessarily a continuous or contiguous one: interruptions are to be expected, some of which are helpful to meditative prayer and others harmful. Were we forced to sustain a constant chatter directed to Christ, meditation would soon become a nerve-racking, wearying occupation. We are at liberty to divide our meditation time into periods of conversation and periods of simple, silent attention to Christ.[4] In these latter periods, the soul contacts Christ without the necessity of recourse to words. When, after a period of this silent contact with Our Lord, attention begins to lag, the verbal (non-expressed words, that is) conversation is to be resumed.

The undesirable form of interrupted conversation is known as distraction. Distractions in the form of imaginative wanderings, day dreams, and mental inattentiveness are to be expected during meditation. The

---

[4] St. Teresa comments: "We must not tire ourselves by going in search of such ideas; we must sometimes remain by His side with our minds hushed in silence." (*Life,* xii) She later adds: "He has no desire that we tire out our brains by a great deal of talking, if only we can realize that we are in His presence . . ." (*Way of Perfection,* xxix)

human mind is a complex mechanism capable of roaming over and probing a vast variety of subjects; and because of this inherent ability and propensity, it requires some effort to direct the attention of the mind to a single subject for any length of time. It will, accordingly, be necessary for one to exercise constant vigilance in returning one's attention to the subject of prayer when distractions assert themselves. However, distractions, their nature and remedies, will be discussed more fully in a later chapter.

The objection might be raised that it is impossible to hold converse with one whom we cannot see visibly. The solution, of course, lies in attempting to make Christ truly present to us by use of our imagination and by the keen insight which faith supplies. St. Teresa disposes of the objection in these words:

> You will ask me how you can possibly do all this, and say that, if you had seen His Majesty with your bodily eyes at the time when He lived in the world, you would have done it willingly and gazed at Him forever. Do not believe it: anyone who will not make the slight effort necessary for recollection in order to gaze upon this Lord present within her, which she can do without danger and with only the minimum of trouble, should have been far less likely to stand at the foot of the cross with the Magdalen.[5]

What shall we say to Christ, what is there to discuss with Him? There is almost an inexhaustible amount of discussion matter for conversation with Our Lord. We can adore Christ, express our love for Him, thank Him for His constant and continued favors, bemoan

[5] St. Teresa, *Way of Perfection*, xxvi.

our sins and faults, petition Him for those things of which we stand in need, discuss our problems with Him.[6] The soul at prayer need never fear that there is lacking suitable conversation material for use with Christ, our friend. If one so desires, he may employ the traditional four ends of prayer—adoration (love), thanksgiving, contrition, petition. In this way, one will inaugurate the conversation with Christ by adoring Him for awhile; then he will pass on to sentiments of thanksgiving, followed after a reasonable time by those of contrition and petition.

This entire section of our meditation period is a highly personal one: each one must speak to Our Lord as his own temperament and disposition dictates. It is almost impossible to give precise directives as to the explicit formulation of our communications with Christ. Each individual pursues his separate career with its attendant joys and difficulties, and, consequently, each will have different things to discuss with Christ. We would consider it a violation of our privacy were someone to suggest an outline for conversation with our parents, friends, or marital partner; it would be equally presumptuous for an outsider to attempt to intrude in the area of personal friendship which exists between Christ and the soul. We are to speak with Our Lord

---

[6] St. Alphonsus states: "There is no barrier at the door against any who desire to speak with Him; nay, God delights that you should treat with Him confidently. Treat with Him of your business, your plans, your griefs, your fears,—of all that concerns you. . . . He would have us often speak with Him familiarly and without restraint." *The Way of Salvation and Perfection* (Brooklyn: Redemptorist Fathers, 1926), pp. 395-6.

as to an intimate friend. Our common experience teaches us the requirements and procedures in ordinary friendly conversation; we are simply asked to apply these concepts to our conversation with Christ.

Our conversations with acquaintances and friends are performed easily, effortlessly, and without strain. Our communications with Christ are also to be conducted in an atmosphere free of tension. Christ does not desire that we struggle and strain to produce affections and sentiments—this would serve to make our meditation period a distasteful daily chore. Instead, we should speak to Our Lord simply and slowly, following the inclination of our present mood and the inspiration of divine grace. If no satisfactory affection seems to be forthcoming on a particular day, we are not to wrestle with ourselves until we squeeze out some sentiment of love or gratitude; on such occasions it will be quite sufficient to acknowledge humbly to Our Lord our weakness and spiritual poverty.

Perhaps much of our diffidence in approaching Christ in this conversational mode stems from the common misconception that prayer is to be employed only when one desires some favor from Christ. Such an erroneous attitude can sadly cripple our contact with Christ. It is true that the prayer of petition is one form of prayer—and a good one at that; but it is not the sole form of prayer, nor even the highest one. We pray principally to arrive at contact with Christ, and to increase our friendship with Him; secondarily, we ask Him trustfully for those things which we need. It would be strange if, for example, we were on terms of close friendship with a man of some wealth, and were to consume entire interviews in petitioning him for some donation: one would rightly suspect that the acquaintance's affluence rather than his friendship were the primary object of our interest in him. So, too, in our dealings with Christ we ought to be primarily interested in Him and only secondarily in what He can do for us. We don't pray to exploit Christ; we pray to express our love for Him. A late, eminent layman of our time has developed this thought graphically:

> Soon I learned that only incidentally is prayer an asking for help. One should have to ask favors of God no oftener than a sensible child asks favors of his father on earth. Prayer is not a slot machine into which you drop a request and a boon falls out of the bottom. We do not pray for help, but oftener we pray for help for others, and even oftener we pray our thanks for blessings already received; above everything else, we pray daily in sheer felicity, in communion, in close contact with the Father, asking nothing whatever but the joy of knowing Him.[7]

And a nun, a modern spiritual writer, continues this thought in her writings:

> A real change in our attitude will only occur when we change the central object of our attention, and when, instead of that object being the self, comes to be God. When, less and less we find ourselves asking God to work miracles for us, and take instead to asking what we can do for Him. When, rather than watching God to see what gift He will produce for us, we begin to wait on God to see what, if anything, we can give to Him.[8]

---

[7] Fulton Oursler, quoted in *The Catholic Digest*, June, 1949.
[8] A Carmelite Nun, *World Without End* (Westminster: Newman), p. 15.

But let us listen to St. Teresa as she reduces these principles to practice, and gives us a glimpse into her own conversation with Christ:

Consider Him bound to the pillar, become the Man of sorrows, all His flesh torn to pieces, enduring this torture for the love He bears you; persecuted by some, covered with spittle by others, forsaken and abandoned by His friends, having nobody to take His part, shivering with cold, and reduced to such absolute solitude that you can, alone and without witnesses, come and mingle your sorrows with His, and console one another . . . You heart will melt with tenderness, in beholding in this state the Divine Spouse of your soul, and if, not satisfied with looking upon Him, you feel interiorly moved to converse with Him, do it; but then be far from you any studied language, make use only of simple words dictated by your heart; they are the most precious to Him. O Lord of the world, and true spouse of my soul, you may say to Him, how comes it that Thou art reduced to such extremity! O my Saviour and my God, can it be that You do not disdain the company of so poor a creature as I, and that I can be of any consolation to You; for it seems to me that I read upon Your countenance that You are consoled in beholding me near You? How can it be Lord, that the angels leave Thee alone and that even Your heavenly Father consoles You not? Since it is thus, my adorable Master, and You have submitted to this excess of suffering for love of me, what is this little that I suffer, and of what can I complain? Confounded at beholding You in this deplorable state, I am resolved henceforth, my dear Master, to suffer all the tribulations that can happen to me, and consider them as treasures in order to imitate You in something. Let us then proceed together, O Lord; I desire to follow You everywhere You go and pass through all that You pass through.[9]

---

[9] St. Teresa, *Way of Perfection,* xxvi.

It should be evident at this point that St. Teresa insists that we talk to God directly during meditation. However, she classifies the period of meditation as a *conversation;* and conversation, in the ordinary acceptance of the word, implies a mutual exchange of words and sentiments. Does Christ respond to our conversation? Does *He* converse with us in prayer? St. Teresa assures us that He most definitely does: meditation is not a monologue, but rather a dialogue. A few texts from the writings of St. Teresa will serve to present a sampling of this fundamental Teresian doctrine:

> Do you suppose that because we cannot hear Him, He is silent? He speaks clearly to the heart when we beg Him from our heart to do so.[10]

> Soon after we have begun to force ourselves to remain near the Lord, He will give us indications that . . . He heard us . . .[11]

> . . . We must be glad that there is no need to raise our voices in order to speak to Him since His Majesty will make us conscious that He is there.[12]

St. Teresa does not intend to infer that this communication from Christ implies any supernatural vision or revelation. Christ speaks to our souls in simple, ordinary ways; and He speaks to all souls to pray to Him— not only to those in the higher regions of the spiritual life. A modern commentator on St. Teresa lucidly describes the manner in which Christ addresses us during meditation:

---

[10] *Ibid.,* xxiv.
[11] *Ibid.,* xxix.
[12] *Ibid.*

St. Teresa teaches us that God does speak to us when we pour out our hearts to Him. We need not think, however, that God makes Himself heard in an audible manner. He answers us by sending us graces of light and of love whereby we understand His ways better and burn with desire to embrace them generously. Listening, therefore, consists in accepting these graces and striving to profit by them.[13]

An eloquent doctor of the Church, and devoted disciple of St. Teresa, discusses the same subject:

> In a word, if you desire to delight the loving heart of your God, be careful to speak to Him as often as you are able, and with the fullest confidence that He will not disdain to answer and speak with you in return. He does not, indeed, make Himself heard in any voice that reaches your ears, but in a voice that your heart can well perceive . . . He will then speak to you by such inspirations, such interior lights, such manifestations of His goodness, such sweet touches in your heart, such tokens of forgiveness, such experience of peace, such hopes of heaven, such rejoicings within you, such sweetnesses of His grace, such loving and close embraces,— in a word, such voices of love—as are well understood by those souls whom He loves, and who seek for nothing but Himself alone.[14]

Hence, if we speak to Christ, we may be consoled that He will speak to us in return.[15] This is why it has

---

[13] Father Gabriel of St. Mary Magdalen, O.C.D., *Little Catechism of Prayer* (Concord, New Hampshire: Discalced Carmelite Nuns, 1949), p. 29.

[14] St. Alphonsus, *The Way of Salvation and Perfection*, p. 408.

[15] In strict theological terminology, we must state that Christ "speaks" to us through the medium of actual graces. He bestows these actual graces upon us to enlighten our intellect and influence our wills. For a clear description of the function of actual grace *cf.* Garrigou-Lagrange, O.P., *The Three Ages of the Interior Life*, Vol. 1, trans. Sister M. Timothea Doyle, O.P. (St. Louis: Herder, 1940), pp. 90-93.

been suggested that during prayer, it is well to vary our verbal conversation directed to Christ with periods of silence, during which we can listen to Him and offer Him our receptivity. We speak to Christ; He speaks to us—we could expect no less of our Divine Friend.

Fortunately, in these days of more frequent Communion, we have become accustomed to establishing personal contact with Christ in our periods of eucharistic thanksgiving. During those few moments following the reception of Holy Communion, many souls definitely talk *with* Christ instead of praying *at* Him. Would that more people would extend this practice of familiar conversation to their meditation periods. Then they would be performing their meditation in the manner desired by St. Teresa—yes, in the manner desired by Christ. At least the practice of post-Communion contact with Christ gives us an introduction to the type of approach which is required in meditation.

The story is related of a small girl who, after the reception of her first Holy Communion, was questioned tenderly by her parents as to what she had done when she arrived back at her pew and bowed her head prayerfully. She hesitated momentarily, and then said in her thin, small voice: "I prayed to Our Lord for Mommy and Daddy, and for my sister Helen, and my brother George; and then I recited the alphabet to Our Lord and told him a ghost story." We, of course, smile indulgently at the naivete and innocence of the small child; but after reflecting on the story, we might suddenly wake to the realization that the girl possessed the proper approach to prayer—*she was actually talking to*

Our Lord. What she said to Christ was relatively unimportant, what she did was decidedly important: she entered into immediate contact with her Friend, Christ. If we could learn to converse with Christ as she did, we would be making successful prayer; if we could adopt her attitude for the conversation period of our meditation, our problems in this regard would be at an end.

It is, therefore, imperative that those who would meditate successfully comprehend and master the essential elements of this part of the procedure. In summary, they are:

1. The soul talks directly *to* Christ.

2. The conversation should be performed slowly and sincerely.

3. It should be phrased in one's own words.

4. The conversation is exercised silently and interiorly—through the use of words (non-expressed) or sentiments of the heart (love, gratitude, etc.).

5. It is to be a protracted conversation, but not necessarily one that is continuous—one should intersperse periods of attentive silence in his conversation.

6. The conversation is sustained without tense, violent efforts to stimulate sentiments and emotions.

7. The conversation with Our Lord is primarily an intimate union of friendship with Him; and only secondarily a petition of benefits from Him.

8. God, in turn, converses with us through the medium of inspirations and illuminations.

CHAPTER

10

THE CONCLUSION
OF THE MEDITATION

AN OLD LATIN AXIOM maintains that the conclusion crowns the work. This is not completely verified in meditative prayer, since the conclusion is an optional step to be employed only if judged useful. However, especially for beginners at prayer, some type of conclusion is generally helpful.

As the end of the daily meditation period draws near, one begins to arrange some sort of finale to his conversation with Christ. It is well that the conversation be not abruptly terminated before it has been rounded off. In a conversation with an acquaintance, it would be considered a breach of etiquette to break off the discussion summarily, and stride rapidly away without some word of farewell; we should endeavor to manifest no less courtesy to Christ.

A fitting conclusion to our meditation period would be a sincere act of gratitude and appreciation offered to

Christ for the privilege of engaging Him in friendly conversation. If we have negotiated a rather successful period of meditation, we ought to thank Him for this also. Acts and sentiments and gratitude always serve as a genteel manner of closing any interview.

One important and extremely advantageous element in the concluding moments of prayer is the brief examination upon the success of the meditation period just completed.[1] This quick, cursory evaluation of the day's meditation serves as a reminder of those defects to be avoided in the future, and presents an incentive to make better prayer in succeeding meditations. One ought not be discouraged if he finds that his meditation has been punctuated with distractions and mental wanderings. He should keep in mind St. Teresa's remarks that "success at prayer is assured";[2] he simply must give it time and effort.

Some authors—particularly St. Francis de Sales[3]— advise that a specific resolution for the general amendment of life be appended to the daily meditation. While this, naturally, is a salubrious thing, it cannot be recommended as a general manner of procedure. First of all, there is some danger that if the resolution be not generated during the actual conversation period, it will be forced and artificial if hastily attached to the conclusion. Then, those who faithfully perform their meditation daily and make some progress in the spiritual life, will find it difficult to invoke new resolutions of a different

---

[1] *Cf.* St. Ignatius, *Exercises,* No. 77.
[2] St. Teresa, *Way of Perfection,* xxiii.
[3] St. Francis de Sales, *Introduction to a Devout Life,* II, 6, 7, 8.

nature each day. It must be noted that St. Francis de
Sales is dealing with absolute beginners in the spiritual
life, and is concerned that their efforts and sentiments
will remain inefficacious if not reduced to practical,
concrete, immediate resolves.[4] Our ordinary conversations with Christ will, from time to time, prompt us to
offer specific resolutions to Him for the amendment of
life. On the other hand, if someone be struggling against
a vice or defect, he might find it helpful during the conclusion of the meditation to formulate briefly once again
his resolve to continue his earnest efforts against it. As
a general rule, though, we may state that the appendage
of a specific resolution to the conclusion of meditation
is not to be advised as a usual practice—if, in individual
cases, it be found useful, then by all means it could be
employed.

The conclusion, therefore, may be completely omitted
as a component element of meditation if it be judged
superfluous in specific cases.[5] However, in most instances, sentiments of gratitude and the examination of
the meditation defects offer a fitting conclusion to our
conversation with Christ. We thank Christ for the
privilege of being with Him; we note our failings during
the meditation, and promise to eradicate them in the
future; we then take a courteous and reluctant leave of
our good Friend.

The meditation period is at an end.

---

[4] *Cf.* Joseph Guibert, S.J., *The Theology of the Spiritual Life* (New
York: Sheed and Ward, 1953), p. 238, for an evaluation of St.
Francis' thought on this matter.

[5] *Cf.* Father Gabriel, *Little Catechism of Prayer*, pp. 13-15, for a
discussion of the optional nature of the conclusion of meditation.

III

Variations of the Method

If anyone tells you there is danger in mental prayer, look upon him as a dangerous enemy, and avoid all contact with him.

—St. Teresa

11

MEDITATIVE RECITATION
OF PRAYERS

S<small>T. TERESA'S METHOD</small> of meditation is an astonishingly facile tool for arriving at successful, rewarding prayer. Her outline will prove for most souls the best possible process for attaining satisfactory results at meditation. The method she advances moves the soul quickly over the preparatory steps into the meaningful conversation with Christ. However, there are some souls—although these be in the great minority—for whom St. Teresa offers a variation of our fundamental method. She presents two alternative methods to be used by those souls who find themselves unable to meditate in the ordinary manner, and by those who, while ordinarily employing the basic method, discover themselves temporarily incapable of exercising it because of extraordinary distractions.

It will be noted as these alternative methods are described that St. Teresa retains her fundamental concept of meditation—conversation with Christ—but she accomplishes it through a different course of action. In her standard method, she demands a stimulation of our intellectual faculties which provide subject matter and incentive for our colloquy with Christ. In the variations, she substitutes other devices in place of intellectual procedure, and produces the conversation through artificial means.

We can only encourage all to test for themselves the suitability of the fundamental method before they turn for relief to one of the two variations. Only a relatively few will be forced to employ the alternative methods as regular procedures. However, even those who are adept at following St. Teresa's usual outline of meditation will occasionally derive sustenance and help from her meditative variations. On some occasions one might, for instance, find himself engulfed with distractions and utterly incapable of retaining his attention on the subject of meditation; he would do well for that day—or for a few days, if it be necessary—to employ one of the two methods to be described. Or, one might be particularly fatigued or emotionally exhausted on a specified day, and consequently be unable to sustain the reflections and ensuing conversation; he, too, will find temporary relief in one of the variations of the fundamental methods.

The first alternative plan—meditative recitation of prayers—will be discussed here; the second—meditative reading—will be described in the following chapter.

When one discovers he is unable to make contact with Christ through the ordinary procedure—either as the result of habitual inability, or temporary indisposition—St. Teresa suggests that he begin slowly and reflectively to recite some familiar vocal prayer: perhaps the "Our Father" or "Hail Mary." This slow recitation of a vocal prayer will serve to place the wandering mind and imagination on a familiar track. The interior faculties which previously were unable to retain a series of thoughts will now be drawn along through the succession of words and phrases of the vocal prayer.

The prayer recited, of course, is not to be dispatched hurriedly as is often done in the daily performance of so many religious practices. The goal desired here is still conversation with God; the vocal prayer is the framework in which that conversation is held. In the method delineated in the previous section of the book, the conversation (a function of the will) was inaugurated after the intellect and imagination had drawn the soul to Christ; in this method, the conversation is begun while the interior faculties are centered on Christ through the instrumentality of the vocal prayer. The over-all process is the same in both instances; the precise development of it differs.

St. Teresa, after commenting on her inability to effect a successful meditation notes:

> I myself spent over fourteen years without being ever able to meditate except while reading. . . . Some find their thoughts wandering so much that they cannot concentrate upon the same thing but are always restless, to such an extent that, if they try to fix their thoughts on God they are attacked by a thousand foolish ideas and scruples and doubts concerning the faith. I know a very old woman, leading a

most excellent life . . . a penitent, and a great servant of
God, who for many years has been spending hours and
hours in vocal prayer, but from mental prayer can get no
help at all; the most she can do is to dwell upon each of her
vocal prayers as she says them. There are a great many other
people just like this; if they are humble, they will not, I
think be any the worse off in the end.[1]

St. Francis de Sales, in describing the fundamental
doctrine of prayer, makes note of this very helpful ancil-
lary method:

Should it happen . . . that you feel no relish or comfort in
meditation, I conjure you not to disturb yourself on that account; but sometimes open the door of your heart to vocal
prayer, complain of yourself to Our Lord, confess your un-
worthiness, and beseech Him to assist you.[2]

St. Therese of Lisieux in her autobiography mentions
that she herself was forced to employ this device:

Sometimes when I am in such a state of spiritual dryness
that not a single good thought occurs to me, I say very
slowly the "Our Father" or the "Hail Mary," and these prayers suffice to take me out of myself, and wonderfully re-
fresh me.[3]

The salient point to be noted here is that the vocal
prayer is recited *meditatively*.[4] Vocal prayers are recited

---

[1] St. Teresa, *Way of Perfection*, xvii.
[2] St. Francis de Sales, *Introduction to a Devout Life*, II, 9.
[3] St. Therese, *Autobiography*, ch. 10.
[4] Father Gabriel in the *Little Catechism of Prayer* describes St.
Teresa's teaching on the meditative recitation of vocal prayers: "St.
Teresa gives another method of controlling thoughts and exciting love
to those whose imaginations and ideas are so volatile that they can only
with the greatest difficulty stop at one idea and reflect on it in an
orderly fashion so as to appreciate its meaning. She urges such souls
to recite very slowly some vocal prayer full of meaning, pausing to

meditatively when they are said slowly, with frequent pauses, and with close attention to the meaning of the prayer. If, by way of example, one is reciting the "Our Father," he might start off by pronouncing the first two words of the prayer; then, he would do well to pause and let the significance of the words penetrate his mind and heart—God is a true Father to us. He would next speak to God, his Father, for as long as he is able to sustain the conversation. When the attention and affections begin to lag, he can move on to the next words of the prayer, repeating the process. It might take ten minutes—or even fifteen or twenty—to complete the prayer in this manner. When the prayer has been concluded, it may be started anew or another prayer selected. It might be quite possible to consume an entire meditation period of one half-hour's duration in repeating the "Our Father" four or five times. The vocal prayer employed here functions as a crutch to sustain the conversation with God. The same principles which guide us in the regular form of meditation are to be applied in the variation: we talk to God sincerely as friend to friend; we enjoy God's companionship; we pause to allow God to converse with us.[5] St. Teresa is careful to note that this meditation device will not necessarily hinder the enjoyment of close union with Christ. She even adds:

> I must tell you that while you are repeating the "Our Father" or some vocal prayer, it is quite possible for the Lord to grant you perfect contemplation.[6]

consider attentively the sense of the words, to reflect upon them and to express their love." (p. 27)

[5] Cf. *supra*, ch. 9, p. 55.

[6] St. Teresa, *Way of Perfection*, xxv.

To support her statement, she cites the case of a nun in her community:

> I know there are many people who practice vocal prayer in the manner already described and are raised by God to higher contemplation . . . I know a nun who could never practice anything but vocal prayer but who kept to this and found she had everything else; yet if she omitted saying her prayers her mind wandered so much that she could not endure it. May we all practice such mental prayer as that. She would say a number of "Our Fathers" . . . and on nothing more than these and a few other prayers she would spend two or three hours. She came to me once in great distress, saying that she did not know how to practice mental prayer, and that she could not contemplate but could only say vocal prayers . . . I asked her what prayers she said, and from her reply I saw that, though keeping to the Our Father, she was experiencing pure contemplation, and the Lord was raising her to be with Him in union.[7]

Therefore, St. Teresa, no less insistent that our meditation be fundamentally a conversation with Christ, supplies us with a new agent for arriving at that goal—meditative recitation of vocal prayers.

---

[7] *Ibid.*, xxx.

CHAPTER

12

MEDITATIVE READING

To the soul unsatisfied by the former methods of meditation, St. Teresa offers a second variant, meditative reading. In this procedure, as in the prior one, the fundamental aim is the procurement of conversation with Christ. But this variant does not utilize the procedures of the two former systems: neither a stimulation of the intellectual powers, nor a meditative recitation of vocal prayers. Instead, the conversation is provoked and sustained by the employment of a book throughout the entire period of meditation.

The precise function of reading in relation to prayer might appear a bit confusing—there are three distinct situations involving the use of reading. It would be well to differentiate them briefly. We have already made mention of the daily spiritual reading so strongly encouraged by spiritual experts. This reading is performed outside the time of prayer; but its connection with prayer, while extremely valuable, is nevertheless indirect. Its function is to supply us with general informa-

79

tion, principles, and data about the spiritual life.[1] Differing from this is the spiritual reading just prior to the inception of the meditation period. This reading serves to select the material for the day's meditation, and to focus one's attention upon it. The book is employed for the few moments anterior to prayer; it is then closed. It may be reopened again to stimulate the interior faculties when attention begins to lag; but its use is an occasional thing.[2] Finally, there remains meditative reading—the subject of this chapter—which St. Teresa presents as a substitute for those unable to meditate in the conventional methods. Here the book is employed as a constant companion throughout the meditation period serving to guide and support one in his conversation with Christ.

St. Teresa suggests this alternative device in these words:

> To use a book written in the vernacular is another very useful means of holding discourse with the Lord. While reading it, your mind will become more easily recollected and you will feel better disposed for prayer.[3]

Her faithful disciple, St. Francis de Sales, takes a cue from St. Teresa in one of his extant letters by offering similar advice:

> Touching meditation, I pray you not to distress yourself, if sometimes, and even very often, you do not find consolation in it; go quietly on, with humility and patience, not on this account doing violence to your spirit. Use your books when you find your soul weary, that is to say, read a little and then meditate, then read again a little and meditate, until the

---

[1] Daily spiritual reading will be discussed more fully in Chapter 21.
[2] *Cf. supra*, ch. 7.
[3] St. Teresa, *Way of Perfection*, xxi.

end of your half-hour. Mother Teresa thus acted in the beginning, and said that she found it a very good plan for herself. And since we are speaking in confidence, I will add that
I have also tried it myself and found it good for me.[4]

One of the early commentators on St. Teresa also
points out the occasional valid use of some form of reading during meditation:

> If, in spite of these precautions, they do not succeed in recol-
> lecting themselves, let them endeavor during the prayer to
> drive away all importunate thoughts. . . . Finally, if notwith-
> standing all, the wandering thoughts continue to disturb
> them, they can use, instead of prayer, spiritual reading ac-
> companied with reflections.[5]

It must be noted that the insistence here is upon
reading *accompanied with reflections.* As in the previous
alternate method, reading is merely intended as a substitute procedure. Instead of arriving at a conversation
with Christ through a stimulation of the intellectual
faculties, the contact with Our Lord is effected and sustained by the use of some book suitable for this purpose.
The book selected is to be read until one finds himself
capable of entering into direct communication with
Christ. The reading of a few sentences will be sufficient
to procure this for some; others will require more—a

---

[4] St. Francis de Sales, *Letters to Persons in Religion,* trans. Henry
Mackey, O.S.B. (Westminster: Newman, 1943), pp. 67 8.

[5] Venerable Father John of Jesus and Mary, O.C.D., *Instruction of
Novices* (New York: Benziger, 1925), p. 235. Father John of Jesus
and Mary (1564–1615), third superior general of the Discalced Carmelites, was one of the most articulate of the early Discalced Carmelite
authors. His writings reflect a penetrating insight into the doctrine of
his contemporaries, and fellow Carmelites, St. Teresa and St. John of
the Cross.

few paragraphs, or pages. When one finds himself able to talk directly to Christ, the book is laid down until its use becomes necessary again. Accordingly, the book is kept at hand throughout the entire period of meditation, although it is not used continuously.

It is necessary that the book employed be one that is conducive to this conversation with Christ. Not all spiritual books—in fact, very few of them—will fit into this category. *The New Testament* is certainly appropriate for meditative reading; so, too, are books containing prayers or sentiments directed to Christ—e.g. St. Alphonsus' *Visits to the Blessed Sacrament*. The book should be carefully chosen and with even greater care than is used in selecting the book employed immediately prior to prayer. The book used before prayer is intended to effect the conversation through an indirect process; the book selected for meditative reading has as its chore the direct production of contact with Christ. But should anyone have on hand *The New Testament* and *The Imitation of Christ,* he will find therein abundant material to work out his meditative reading.

If, for example, one were to employ St. Alphonsus' *Visits to the Blessed Sacrament,* he might read these sentences:

> Drive from me every love which is not for Thee, every desire which displeases Thee, every thought which does not tend towards Thee. My Jesus, my love, my treasure, my all, I am determined to please Thee alone. I will give pleasure only to Thee. Thou alone deserve all my heart; Thee alone will I love with all my heart.[6]

---

[6] St. Alphonsus Liguori, *Visits to the Most Blessed Sacrament,* Twenty-first visit.

Then, closing the book, he would repeat these sentiments to Christ in his own words, attempting to formulate them with the greatest degree of sincerity and personal conviction. If it be possible, the ideal is to use the
sentiments of the book as a starter for his own personal
affections. But, at the very least, one may use the words
of the saint as a model upon which to pattern his own
conversation with Christ.

St. Teresa offers us some comfort by informing us that
for many years she performed her meditation through
the instrumentality of reading:

> During all these years, except after communicating, I never
> dared to begin to pray without a book. . . . It seemed to me,
> in these early stages of which I am speaking, that provided
> I had books and could be alone, there was no risk of my
> being deprived of that great blessing.[7]

The value of meditative reading can be readily understood: it brings the wandering attention into direct contact with Christ, and sustains it when it again begins to
falter. Some few souls will find that meditative reading
must, perforce of personal temperament, be their regular
system of meditation; most souls will be forced to rely
upon meditative reading only on occasional intervals.

The one important admonition to be stressed here is
the warning that meditative reading is not to degenerate
into simple spiritual reading. Father Gabriel comments
on this:

> We must be on our guard, however, not to change medita-
> tion into mere reading. Prayer should remain at least medi-

---

[7] St. Teresa, *Life,* iv.

tative reading, during which we pause from time to time to make affections and resolutions. Then reading itself becomes an instrument, an aid to our conversation with God.[8]

Meditative reading in its most fundamental stage would consist in reading a few lines, pausing a few seconds to speak directly to Christ, and then repeating the procedure of reading and praying throughout the entire period of meditation. In its most advanced stage, meditative reading would entail reading for a few seconds, and then talking to Christ for a considerable length of time before it becomes necessary to resume the reading. But in either case, the reading is not the important element; the conversation with Christ is paramount.

---

[8] Father Gabriel, O.C.D., *Little Catechism of Prayer*, p. 22.

IV

Difficulties
in Meditation

He gave me courage to practice mental prayer. I say, courage, because I know nothing in the world that requires more of this.

—St. Teresa

CHAPTER

13

DISTRACTIONS

IT WOULD BE NAIVE to maintain that St. Teresa's
method of meditation immediately solves all the problems of mental prayer. St. Teresa herself is quick to
note the distractions and aridities which vex one continually during meditation. She would at the outset remind those who undertake the practice of meditation
that distractions and aridities are the perennial, provoking
problems encountered by all. Therefore, any realistic
approach to the question of meditation must, of necessity, come to grips with these problems.

It is essential for beginners at meditation to realize
that distractions and aridities are a constant annoyance
to be expected without surprise. Else, one might eagerly
undertake St. Teresa's method of meditation, and then,
when distractions make their presence felt, abandon entirely the habit of meditation. No one can entirely avoid
distractions at prayer; he can, however, diminish them,
and develop a mature attitude in coping with them. It
will, accordingly, be the burden of this chapter to equip

the beginner at prayer with the proper mentality in
dealing with these hazards of meditation.

Distractions and aridities are commonly presented as
identical elements having only terminological differ-
ences. However, as will be demonstrated, distractions
and aridities represent two distinct areas of difficulty:
distractions affect the intellect, and aridities harass the
will. When one is distracted his mind wanders from
the subject of meditation; when he suffers aridity his
will receives no consolation in conversing with Christ.
Distractions will be discussed here, and aridities in the
following chapter.

St. Teresa presents her doctrine of meditation in au-
tobiographical fashion: she not only demonstrates the
principles of prayer, but she portrays the elements and
difficulties of prayer as they transpired in her own life.
Hence, she paints graphically for us the annoying distractions which were hers during prayer:

> I suffered great trials in prayer, for the spirit was not master
> in me, but slave. I could not, therefore, shut myself up
> within myself . . . without at the same time shutting in a
> thousand vanities. I spent many years in this way . . .[1]

> Very often over a period of several years I was more occu-
> pied in wishing my hour of prayer were over, and in listen-
> ing whenever the clock struck, than in thinking of things
> that were good. Again and again I would rather have done
> any severe penance that might have been given me than
> practice recollection as a preliminary to prayer. . . . When-
> ever I entered the oratory I used to feel so depressed that I had
> to summon up all my courage to make myself pray at all.[2]

---

[1] St. Teresa, *Life*, vii.
[2] *Ibid.*, viii.

Those of you whose minds cannot reason for long or whose thoughts cannot dwell upon God but are constantly wandering must at all costs form this habit. I know quite well that you are capable of it—for many years I endured this trial of being unable to concentrate on one subject, and a very sore trial it is.[3]

This is certainly consolation for us who find such intense difficulty and repugnance in prayer from time to time. How apart from the caricature of the saints we so often meet is this personal glimpse into St. Teresa's own prayer life. We are accustomed to think that the saints experienced none of our common difficulties at prayer, that their meditations were untrammeled periods of repose in God. St. Teresa quickly dissipates this false notion. The saints at prayer were often in troubled waters—can we expect any less?

Abstracting from her own case, St. Teresa presents an objective picture of a typical soul distressed by distractions:

We are meditating on the nature of the world, and on the way in which everything will come to an end, and so that we may learn to despise it, when almost without noticing it, we find ourselves ruminating on things in the world that we love. We try to banish these thoughts, but we cannot help being slightly distracted by thinking of things that have happened, or will happen, of things we have done and of things we are going to do. Then we begin to think of how we can get rid of these thoughts; and that sometimes plunges us once again into the same danger.[4]

We can only too readily affirm that this is a valid

[3] St. Teresa, *Way of Perfection*, xxvi.
[4] *Ibid.*, xix.

Conversation with Christ

representation of a soul at prayer. We begin our meditation with high hopes of engaging Christ in personal, heart-to-heart conversation, and almost before we realize it, we are enmeshed in a web of distracting thoughts and memories. Sometimes we can quite readily dismiss these intruding thoughts and continue our meditation; but more often there seems to be no relief from the distractions which insinuate themselves into our prayer. How, then, do we cope with this problem? ✓

First of all, we must distinguish carefully between voluntary and involuntary distractions. A distraction, in general, is the intrusion of thoughts foreign to the subject of meditation. Voluntary distractions are those which are wilfully introduced, or entertained after their presence is apprehended. Contrary-wise, involuntary distractions are those which are not wilfully incited, nor willingly retained after their discovery. Involuntary distractions are more our concern here; for voluntary distractions partake of the nature of an infidelity rather than a difficulty. Those who entertain voluntary distractions are guilty of venial sin insofar as they commit an act of irreverence to God.

It will be impossible to eradicate involuntary distractions entirely; but we can lessen their number and intensity so as to prohibit them from depriving our meditation of its beneficial results. Since our distractions arise from many sources, it will be necessary to employ different techniques on their various causes. The sources of distractions are manifold: exterior sensations and visual images, lack of preparation, failure in recollection, vivid and unstable imagination, ill-restrained passions, weak health, excessive fatigue. Hence, each type of distraction calls for a specific remedy. Those distractions which arise from an exterior source can be combatted by a more careful vigilance over our senses during the time of prayer; those which originate from interior causes present greater difficulties.

Here again individual temperament must be taken into consideration. Some souls are of a volatile and highly imaginative disposition: it is difficult for them to retain their attention upon any subject for a fixed amount of time. Others are of a nature inclined to brood over their difficulties and failures: they will bring this attitude of mind—plus their preoccupying thoughts —to prayer. Again, others possess a dull, listless temperament which thrusts them into frequent periods of lethargic dreaminess: they will find that meditation has a soporific affect upon them. And so the list could be continued. It is only of importance to remember that we all possess distinct temperaments, and they must be directed and remedied in diverse ways.

However, even after our distractions have been combatted indirectly through an intensification of our love for Christ and a mastery over our interior faculties, and directly through an intense reapplication to the subject of meditation, we may yet find ourselves harassed by many disturbing thoughts. Is there any remedy for these? Practically speaking, there is not: we must simply endure them. If we have diligently attempted to purge our distractions by the direct and indirect methods, and they still remain, there is nothing to be gained by becoming saddened or upset at their presence. Patience with ourselves is the attitude of mind called for here.

Many lose their peace of mind in discovering that their prayer is fraught with distractions over which they seem to have little control. St. Teresa takes pains to mention frequently in her writings that involuntary distractions which cannot be dismissed should give no cause for concern:

> I repeat my advice . . . that one must never be depressed or afflicted because of aridities or unrest or distraction of the mind. If a person would gain spiritual freedom and not be continually troubled, let him begin by not being afraid of the cross and he will find that the Lord will help him to bear it; he will then advance happily and find profit in everything.[5]

> There are occasions when one cannot help doing this: times of ill health . . . or times when our heads are tired, and however hard we try, we cannot concentrate. . . . The very suffering of anyone in this state will show her that she is not to blame, and she must not worry, for that only makes matters worse, nor must she worry herself by trying to put sense into something—namely, her mind—which for the moment is without any.[6]

Yes, St. Teresa is right: there are occasions when, despite our earnest efforts, we can in no way dispel our distractions. St. Teresa cautions us not to become careless in dispelling them, but to continue to meditate as best we can—despite the distractions—with the hope that we will experience better days at prayer in the future. The prime danger here is that one may become so dismayed by his failure to reject distractions that he aban-

---

[5] St. Teresa, *Life*, x.
[6] St. Teresa, *Way of Perfection*, xxiv.

dons the practice of meditation: that would be sheer tragedy.

Nor must we imagine that meditation laden with distractions is displeasing to God. St. Teresa comments:

> When the understanding ceases to work, they cannot bear it, even though perhaps the will is increasing in power, and attaining new strength, without their knowing it. We must realize that the Lord pays no heed to these things: to us they may look like faults, but they are not so. His Majesty knows our wretchedness and the weakness of our nature better than we ourselves, and He knows that all the time these souls are longing to think of Him and to love Him. It is this determination that He desires in us.[7]

All that God desires is this determination of which St. Teresa speaks. If we struggle along with our meditation in the face of constant distractions, we may be consoled that such prayer is most pleasing to God.

St. Alphonsus dramatically pleads the cause for perseverance at meditation, irrespective of persistent distractions:

> Let us remember that the devil labors hard to disturb us at the time of meditation, in order to make us abandon it. Let him, then, who omits mental prayer on account of distractions be persuaded that he gives delight to the devil . . . let us, then, never give up meditation however great our distractions may be. St. Francis de Sales says that if, in mental prayer, we should do nothing else than continually banish distractions and temptations, the meditation would be well made. Before him, St. Thomas taught that involuntary distractions do not take away the fruit of mental prayer.[8]

---

[7] St. Teresa, *Life*, xi.

[8] St. Alphonsus, *The Great Means of Salvation and Perfection*, p. 281.

Distractions, therefore, present a serious problem for those engaging in daily meditation. Anyone who would persevere in meditation must be prepared to encounter this difficulty. In summation, these are the principal facts to be borne in mind as distractions begin to assert themselves:

1. Distractions are the common experience of *all* who practice mental prayer.

2. Distractions can—and must—be lessened and reduced.

3. Distractions, however, cannot be entirely eradicated.

4. Distractions must not discourage the soul from perseverance at meditation.

Accordingly, we carry with us to meditation two vital attitudes of mind, determination and patience: determination to remove those distractions which can be eradicated, patience to endure those which cannot be dismissed.

CHAPTER

14

ARIDITIES

THE PRESENCE of aridities during meditation offers a more complex problem than mere distractions. The soul suffering from aridities discovers that he experiences no consolation or satisfaction in his conversation with Christ. In fact, he may find the entire practice of meditation severly repugnant. This presents greater difficulty than simple lack of attention at prayer; for the temptation to discontinue sterile meditation is a more pressing one.

St. Teresa candidly describes for us one of her periodic moods of aridity—the common fortune of all who follow Christ:

> Sometimes, though not often, for perhaps three, four or five days on end, I feel as if all good thoughts and reverent impulses and visions are leaving me, and are vanishing from my memory, so that I cannot recall anything good that there has ever been in me even if I wish. Everything seems like a dream—or, at least—I can remember nothing of it. And in addition to all of this I am pressed by bodily pains: my understanding is troubled, so that I cannot think in the very least

about God and have no idea under what law I am living. If I read, I cannot understand what I am reading; I seem to be full of faults and am not courageous enough to be virtuous, and the courage of which I used to have plenty has sunk so low that I feel I should be unable to resist the smallest of the temptations or slanders of the world. At such a time I get the idea that if I am to be employed for anything beyond the most ordinary matters I shall be useless. I grow sad, thinking I have deceived everyone who has any belief in me; I want to be able to hide myself where nobody can see me; and my desire for solitude is the result, no longer a virtue but a pusillanimity. I feel that I should like to quarrel with all who oppose me.[1]

Nor is it to be imagined that this frank confession is the cry of one enmeshed in a life of sin—St. Teresa at the time of this writing had already reached some of the highest stages of the spiritual life. The value of this bit of self-revelation is that it reminds us to expect occasional stretches of aridity throughout our entire life.

The same general procedure as was applied to distractions is to be employed upon aridities: eliminate those we can, and patiently bear those we cannot.

Aridity, which may be defined as the withdrawal of consolation and enthusiasm in loving Christ, is best combatted by attacking its causes. There are three principal sources of aridity: a lack of full development in the spiritual life; inculpable circumstances; the purifying action of God.

The first main source of aridity—lack of full development in the spiritual life—is combatted by strengthening and developing our love for Christ. If one is seriously

---

[1] St. Teresa, *Spiritual Relations*, No. 1.

attached to sin or things of this world, he will, naturally, derive less satisfaction from companionship with Christ. It is a fundamental psychological law that we enjoy the presence of that which we love: if we love Christ, we will enjoy His presence, but if we are not fully enamored of Christ, we will experience some degree of weariness in praying to Him. Our Lord Himself commented on this basic rule of human nature: ". . . where thy treasure is, there thy heart also will be." [2] Accordingly, if we are still involved in venial sin, or tepidity, or mediocrity, we will suffer aridity in meditation. The solution to the problem lies in extirpating this tepidity from our life.

The second source of aridity—involuntary circumstances—is less easily handled. This source includes: illness, physical fatigue, drowsiness, worries, absorbing preoccupations, misunderstandings, and temptations. These again are to be eradicated or lessened insofar as it lies in our power. Most often there is not much that can be done to combat aridities from this source; but we do what we can, and then patiently endure the aridities which remain.

The third cause of arid meditation—the purifying action of God—represents a phenomena encountered by those whom God is leading to the higher stages of prayer. To prepare some for a life of closer union with him, God purifies their souls by a period devoid of sense consolation. This will be discussed more fully in a later chapter. We prefer to abstract completely from this

[2] Matt., 6, 21.

species of aridity in the present discussion, for our consideration of meditation up to this point has embraced only the ordinary ways of prayer.[3]

The attitude of mind St. Teresa would have us bring to the problem of aridity is mainly one of generous acceptance of this trial. She would remind us that the mark of a true follower of Christ is willingness to serve without recompense—or in this case, consolation at prayer. She writes:

> Once we have made a habit of thinking of Him in this way, it becomes very easy to find Him at our side, though there will come times when it is impossible to do either the one thing or the other. For that reason it is advisable to do as I have already said: we must not show ourselves to be striving after spiritual consolations; come what may, the great thing for us to do is to embrace the cross. The Lord was deprived of all consolations; they left Him alone in His trials. Let us not leave Him.[4]

To serve even when there is no delight in serving: this is true love. And St. Teresa demands this brand of love from those who would gain profit from the practice of meditation. She continues:

> I fear (the soul) will never attain the true poverty of spirit, which consists in seeking, not comfort or pleasure in prayer . . . but consolation and trials for the love of Him who suffered trials all His life long; and we must endure these trials, and be calm amidst aridities, though we may feel some regret at having to suffer them. They should not cause us the unrest and distress which they cause some people who think that, if they are not forever laboring with their understand-

---

[3] Cf. chapter 21.
[4] St. Teresa, *Life,* xxii.

ing and striving after feelings of devotion, they are going completely astray.[5]

St. Teresa in no wise intends to infer that those who meditate must necessarily be constantly harassed by aridities. In the ordinary unfolding of God's plan, aridity is an occasional experience. Human enthusiasm in any field cannot be maintained at the same constant pitch: we must expect a rise and fall in our appreciation of any object in life. No less is to be expected of our conversation with Christ. St. Teresa would have us expect this phenomena of life, and continue perseveringly in our meditation until the mood passes—whether this entail a few hours, or a few days.

Aridity in our meditation presents us with an excellent opportunity for demonstrating unselfish love for Christ, a love that does not require consolation to sustain it. St. Teresa comments:

> Perhaps we do not know what love is: it would not surprise me a great deal to learn this, for love consists, not in the extent of our happiness, but in the firmness of our determination to try to please God in everything, and to endeavor, in all possible ways, not to offend Him, and to pray Him ever to advance the honor and glory of His Son and the growth of the Catholic Church. Those are the signs of love; do not imagine that the important thing is never to be thinking of anything else and that if your mind becomes slightly distracted all is lost.[6]

In fact, God uses our periods of aridity to draw us to a more mature, unselfish love of Himself. St. Alphonsus develops this thought:

---

[5] *Ibid.*

[6] St. Teresa, *Interior Castle*, IV, i.

The greatest pains of souls in meditation is to find themselves sometimes without a feeling of devotion, weary of it,
and without any sensible desire of loving God. . . . When a
soul gives itself up to the spiritual life, the Lord is accustomed to heap consolations upon it, in order to wean it from
the pleasures of the world, but afterwards, when He sees it
more settled in spiritual ways, He draws back His hand in
order to make proof of His love and to see whether it serves
and loves God unrecompensed, while in this world, with
spiritual joys. Some foolish persons seeing themselves in the
state of aridity, think that God may have abandoned them;
or, again, that the spiritual life was not made for them; and
so they leave off prayer, and lose all that they have gained.[7]

Thus, when the soul feels no consolation at meditation—rather, a weariness in conversing with Christ—he
should simply draw near to Our Lord, remain in His
presence, and offer Him the unparalleled gift of a generous, selfless love. St. Francis de Sales charmingly
draws a simile between a soul beset by aridities and a
courtier in a king's palace:

But if, after all, you should receive no comfort, be not dis-
turbed, no matter how excessive the dryness may be; but
continue to remain in a devout posture in the presence of
God. How many courtiers enter a hundred times a year into
the king's presence chamber without hopes of speaking to
him, but merely to be seen by him, and to pay him their
homage. So ought we . . . to come to holy prayer, purely and
merely to pay our homage, and testify our fidelity to God.
Should it please His Divine Majesty to speak to us and entertain Himself with us by His holy inspirations and interior consolations, it would certainly be an honor above our
merits, and the source of the sweetest consolation; but should

---

[7] St. Alphonsus, *The Great Means of Salvation and Perfection*, p.
282.

it not please Him to grant us this favor, but leave us without taking any more notice of us as if we were not in His presence, we must not therefore depart, but continue with respect and devotion in presence of His adorable Majesty. Observing our diligence, our patience, and perseverance, He will, when we come again before Him, favor us with His consolations, and make us experience the sweetness of His holy prayer.[8]

Aridity, of course, is a sometime thing. But it presents a splendid occasion for developing a true love of Christ. If our periodic sessions of arid prayer are accepted, not so much as a trial, but rather as an opportunity, they will serve to enhance our future meditations and enrich our entire spiritual life.[9]

---

[8] St. Francis de Sales, *Introduction to a Devout Life*, II, 9.

[9] We do not intend to disparage the use of spiritual consolations in the spiritual life. It is entirely proper to seek these consolations as an aid to spiritual progress; however, they should be sought with discretion and resignation. And if one be deprived of them, he will possess an opportunity of serving God without any immediate reward.

V

Demonstration of the Method

I confess that I never knew what it was to pray with satisfaction until the Divine Master Himself deigned to teach me such a salutary method.

—St. Teresa

15

THE REGULAR METHOD—
A DEMONSTRATION

THE NEOPHITE at meditation avidly grasps any shred
of information which might facilitate his own
prayer. It would certainly be advantageous to him if he
were somehow able to eavesdrop upon the meditation
of one who has grasped the principles of sound meditation. This is, of course, impossible: meditative prayer
lies beyond the range of audio-sensory perception. In
lieu of that, it might be helpful if we here attempt to
describe a typical meditation as it would be made by
an average soul.

Such an attempt suffers severe limitations. It is, first
of all, highly artificial: no one can with complete fidelity
and candor express sentiments of heart on paper. In
fact, the deeper sentiments of life defy expression: who,
for example, can adequately articulate the emotions entailed in a warm handclasp with a treasured friend?
Secondly, a written account of a meditation must, of

necessity, exclude any portrayal of those periods of silent attention to Christ which are interspersed throughout a well-made meditation. Nor can any description be given of Christ's response to our conversation with Him as was discussed in Chapter 9. However, despite these very definite handicaps, and with an admonition that they be kept in mind throughout, we will endeavor to act out a model meditation.

(GENERAL PREPARATION) I am about to embark upon a new experience—meditation. I have never made a formal meditation prior to this. But I am determined to begin—and continue—this invaluable exercise of the spiritual life. I know that if I do my part, success is assured.

(IMMEDIATE PREPARATION) I am alone in my room. I kneel and beg God's forgiveness for all my infidelity of the past— "O, my God, I am heartily sorry. . . ."

I am here; but Christ also is here. He is nearer to me than any other person in the world; and in this awareness of Our Lord's presence, all my other concerns and cares fade away. Only two people in the world exist at this moment—Christ and myself. Nothing else is important.

I pause to let the fact of Christ's nearness sink into my consciousness. I raise my face to Him. I am alone with my Divine Friend.

(READING) My copy of *The New Testament* is at hand; I open it to the twenty-third chapter of the Gospel of St. Luke—the account of Christ's crucifixion. I read it slowly and attentively.

(IMAGINATION) After a few minutes of reading I lay the book down, close my eyes, and attempt to depict the scene of the crucifixion in my imagination. I see the slight hill of Golgotha outside Jerusalem with people milling over its gradual ascents. There are the gayly clad Jewish men and women worked up to a feverish pitch of excitement; there are the Roman soldiers, cold and efficient in their gleaming armor; and there is Christ —pinned to the bulky cross, bleeding, suffering, but majestic. All these are there; but I am there too. I move over near the base of the cross. I look up at the face of Christ; it is begrimed with dirt and sweat and blood. His beard hangs matted upon His chin; His lips are thick and swollen. But His eyes—ah, His eyes—are tender, kind, and hurt. While I gaze upwards, the cross creaks gently in the afternoon breeze, and Christ quickly sucks in air as the weight of His body tears against the wounds in His hands. Yes, I am on Calvary with Christ.

(CONSIDERATION) Now I must reflect briefly on this scene so as to lead myself into conversation with Our Lord. I will ask myself some of the traditional meditation questions: who? what? and why? *Who* is it that suffers here: It is Christ, true God and true man. This is not some malefactor apprehended in crime, this is the all-good, all-holy God. This is Jesus who came to earth to offer heaven to men—and now they are cruelly crushing out His life. This bleeding, groaning, dying man is my God.

What is happening? Christ, my God, is being executed in one of the most painful Roman capital punishments, crucifixion. The burly soldiers stretched Our
Lord on the wooden beams of the crucifix, and with
hammer and spikes actually nailed Him to the wood.
They hoisted the cross—the wood and its attached victim
—into an upright position; then they allowed it to slide
into the prepared slot, dragging the full weight of
Christ's body onto the wounds of His hands and feet.
And there He hung—in that awful, fearful silence.

Why is this happening? The fact that it is God who
suffers these torments is, at first consideration, an insolu-
ble mystery. The Lord of heaven and earth allows His
own creatures to inflict these punishments upon Him:
astonishing! But as I turn it over in my mind, the whole
situation becomes distressingly clear. Christ is suffering
for the sins of mankind; He is redeeming men from the
fate prepared for them by their cheap and shabby faults.
He is graphically and dramatically portraying for us the
hideous nature of personal sin. And more than this: Our
Lord in His death presents to us tangible proof of His
love for each and every one of us. Did He not previously
proclaim: "Greater love than this no man has than that
he lay down his life for his friend." Christ is suffering
for the sins of mankind; He is suffering for *my* sins: He
is suffering to prove His love for me.

(CONVERSATION)   Up to this point I have been a mute
spectator on Calvary, but now I am ready to inaugurate
my conversation with Christ. I look up again at the tired

face of my Lord, and slowly, gently speak to Him. Dear Jesus, I feel so sorry for You, so terribly saddened at the tortures You have chosen to undergo. Can I offer You some small consolation by telling You that I deeply and gratefully appreciate all You are doing for me. Thank You, Jesus.

I bitterly regret all my sins which have been the cause of Your agony. At the time of the commission of my many sins, I was only concerned with the pleasure and satisfaction I could derive from them; the sadness they caused Your heart did not in the least trouble me. Now, standing in the shadow of the cross, I view things in a new light: sin is not delightful, it is horrible. I firmly promise You—with Your help, for I am so weak—to eradicate sin from my life. You have stated that if we love You, we will keep Your commandments. I do love You, Jesus, and I do want to obey Your commandments.

"Greater love than this no man has . . ." Yes, Jesus, You have demonstrated to me beyond any shadow of a doubt that You deeply and truly love me. Your wounds are trophies of Your love for me. Can I ever doubt of Your love, Your tender concern for me? I, on my part, must reciprocate this love: I must constantly and continually demonstrate my affection and regard for You.

I delight in having found so good a friend in You, Christ. All my other loves and affections pale in the face of this tremendous love existing between You and me. I love you, Jesus; I love you above all other persons and things.

In this intimacy of heart between Christ and myself,

I pause, gazing upon Him, and silently offer my love to Him. I continue in this attitude of affectionate attention to Christ for some minutes; but soon distracting thoughts protrude themselves into my mind—I have lost contact with Christ.

According, I open the Gospels again and read further in the account of the crucifixion—the incident of the good thief on the cross arrests my attention . . . "Amen, I say to you that this day you shall be with me in paradise." I close the book and renew my conversation with Christ.

Jesus, You are thoughtful and considerate to this poor criminal even in the moment of Your most intense anguish. This incident lays open to me new facets of the basic goodness of You. I, too, like the good thief, stand in need of pardon, and a promise of heaven. The compelling desire of my life is that one day You may say to me: "This day you shall be with Me in paradise." I ardently desire to live in paradise with You and enjoy the wonder of Your companionship forever. As I stand here looking up into Your tired eyes soon to close in death, I want to assure You of three things: my sincere sorrow for my past, my abiding love for You, and my heartfelt desire to live with You in paradise.

(CONCLUSION) The time allotted for my meditation is coming to a rapid close. I want to thank You, Jesus, for allowing me to spend these moments of companionship with You. I sincerely appreciate the assistance you have given me to negotiate a successful meditation.

Looking quickly back over my meditation, I note some

failings insofar as I was remiss in promptly banishing distractions. I promise a greater diligence in the future.

"Lord, remember me when You shall have come into Your kingdom." Good mother, Mary: pray for me. Amen.

CHAPTER

16

THE ALTERNATE METHODS — A DEMONSTRATION

Following the same general course of action utilized in the preceding chapter, we will here enact a demonstration of the two alternative methods of meditation described above in Part III. These artificial meditations will, of necessity, contain the same serious handicaps as did the former one; but they will serve to present a practical demonstration of the principles previously enunciated.

(I) MEDITATIVE RECITATION OF PRAYERS: I am experiencing some difficulty today in retaining my attention upon the subject of my meditation. The wanderings of mind which I now suffer are more troublesome than my usual daily distractions; hence, I feel it would be advantageous to apply one of the alternative methods. I will choose meditative vocal prayer—and I will employ the "Our Father."

Our Father . . . In teaching us this prayer, Dear Lord, You remind us at the outset that You wish to be known and loved as a father. You desire no impersonal relationship with Your creatures; rather, You invite us to the intimacy enjoyed between a father and his child.

You make it quite easy for me to comprehend the relationship which must exist between us. I well know the nature of a father's love for his child; I am personally acquainted with a number of excellent parents. I simply recall the concepts I have acquired about human parents and apply them to You, my Divine Parent. Yes, You are my father; and I love You with a child's tender, trusting love.

Who art in heaven . . . You live in heaven; but is this the limit of Your presence—no! You are omnipresent; You follow me wherever I go; I can never hide from You. But it is in heaven that You will manifest Yourself to me in a special way.

In this prayer, You dangle before my eyes the promise of a paradise. Help me, O Lord, to be faithful to You so that I may one day enjoy the full experience of Your companionship in that home of unending pleasure—heaven.

Hallowed be Thy name . . . Father, my principal occupation on earth should be the worship of Your glory. Men forget, for the most part, that they possess a solemn obligation to adore and revere You. I will attempt, in some small way, to make up this deficit by a warm, loving, affectionate response to You.

Thy kingdom come . . . I desire with all my heart the spread of Your kingdom on earth; and I promise to do all I am able to increase the growth of Your Church. Here is an opportunity for me to do something positive for You: labor for the extension of Your kingdom. Men so often approach You only to receive gifts from You; they fail to appreciate that they, in turn, must do things for You. This is an obligation . . . and a privilege. I will in the future spare myself no effort when an opportunity of working for You presents itself.

Thy will be done . . . Your Divine Son clearly affirmed that not everyone who says, 'Lord, Lord' will enter the kingdom of heaven; no, only those who comply with Your Will. The prime aspect of Your Will in my regard is that I avoid sin. Sin is diametrically opposed to Your wishes. I have sinned in the past, my good Father, but I intend in the future—with Your help—to extirpate sin from my life. *Genuine Humility*

Give us this day our daily bread . . . I am utterly dependent upon You for all the necessities of my spiritual and material life. Without Your constant support I would fall into nothingness. Mindful of this, I once again humbly petition You for everything of which I stand in need—be it temporal or spiritual.

Forgive us our trespasses . . . O God, be merciful to me a sinner. I have sinned; and You know it so well. But I have confidence that Your mercy far exceeds my sinfulness.

from the heart

As we forgive those who trespass against us . . . You place this important restriction upon the pardon of my sins: that I exhibit the same forgiveness to my fellowmen that I expect You to bestow on me. It would be unthinkable to demand pardon from You, and at the same time refuse that pardon to people who have offended me. Hence, Father, I do forgive all who have in any way injured me. I bear no grudges against them; I will be kind in my dealings with them.

Lead us not into temptation, but deliver us from evil . . . I am buffeted on many sides, good Father, with temptations to disobey Your law and grow lax in Your service. I need Your powerful assistance, else I will be consumed by these temptations. Help me, my God.

The time assigned for my meditation has not yet been completed. Therefore, I will begin anew to recite the "Our Father" meditatively; or I shall select a different prayer—perhaps the "Hail Mary." At any rate, I will continue to hold converse with God, through the assistance of some vocal prayer, until the period of meditation is terminated.

(II) Meditative Reading: Today—when meditation has proven unusually difficult—I will seek support from one of the alternate methods. I will enlist the aid of meditative reading. I have selected as my book *The Imitation of Christ*. I turn to Book II, Chapter 7, and begin to read the section entitled, "The Love of Jesus Above All Things."

For Perspective

"Blessed is he who knows what it is to love Jesus and

Jesus said to love the Lord, thy God, with all your mind, heart, soul and strength and your neighbor as yourself. He also said, "Love one another as I (Jesus) have loved you."

These are the greatest commandments with Loving God as the First & greatest of all commandments.

to despise himself for the sake of Jesus. We must quit
what we love for this Beloved, because Jesus will be
loved alone above all things." . . . Yes, Jesus, You are
to be the love of my life, the only important concern in
everything I do. Loving You will entail sacrifices: I must
often relinquish what is pleasurable so that I may continue in Your friendship. You demand my whole heart,
You require that I love You above all things. And I pro-
pose to live up to Your plans for me.

"The love of Jesus is faithful and enduring. He that
cleaveth to creatures shall fall with them. He that em-
braceth Jesus shall stand firm forever. Love Him and
keep Him for thy friend, who, when all go away, will
not leave thee nor suffer thee to perish in the end." . . .
All my other friends will one day leave me, Jesus. Only
You will endure—constant and unrelenting in Your
friendship for me. So many of my loves and friendships
tend to draw me away from You; they place grave
obstacles to our mutual companionship. I reject all such
loves. If I adhere to baser loves, they will one day de-
stroy me; but if I attach myself firmly to You, I will be
lifted up and one day enjoy the full measure of Your
companionship in paradise.

"Keep thyself with Jesus both in life and in death and
commit thyself to His care, who alone can help thee
when all others fail." . . . You are the most powerful
friend a person could have—who else could promise
paradise as a reward for friendship? You not only offer
me a reward, but You also continually aid me in sustaining my friendship with You. And I know that when

all my other friends have failed me, when I shall be of no use to anyone else, Your love will be as constant and true as it is today.

"The Beloved is of such a nature that He will admit of no other, but will have thy heart to Himself, and sit there like a king upon his own throne." . . . You desire my whole heart, Jesus, not just a portion of it. But, after all, it is of the nature of friendship and love to demand exclusive affection from the one loved. To keep any segment of my heart from You would be infidelity. May no love or desire ever come between us, Lord.

"If thou couldst but purge thyself well from affection to creatures, Jesus would willingly dwell with thee. Thou wilt find all that in a manner lost, which thou hast placed in men apart from Jesus." . . . Every corner of my life which is not permeated with love for You, Jesus, is wasted effort. If I could but eradicate all my frivolous desires, I could live much closer to You. Help me, my Good Friend, to extirpate from my life all that hinders my love for You.

My eye runs down the page, and I continue reading: *"For a man does himself more harm if he seeks not Jesus, than the whole world and all his enemies could do."* . . . This is something of which I must convince myself and work into the very fabric of my life: that the most grave evil which could befall me is separation from You. Permit me never to be separated from You. You are my friend; You are my only true friend. Jesus, I love You.

I have rapidly completed this short chapter of the *Imitation*. I may now run through the same chapter again, or advance on to the next section, Chapter 8. And in this manner—reading and talking to Christ—I will continue my meditation to its conclusion.

VI

Indispensable Aids
to Meditation

> The devil knows that he has
> lost the soul that persever-
> ingly practices mental prayer.
>
> —St. Teresa

17

RECOLLECTION: *The Presence of God*

> *→ having one meaning only*

THE SPIRITUAL LIFE is an univocal whole—we cannot plan to augment one part of it while neglecting the rest. And, conversely, we cannot become deficient in a single area without detriment to the entire structure. Therefore, any attempt to stress individual virtues with the positive exclusion of other virtues is doomed to failure. With these reservations in mind, we will in this section describe three virtues and practices of the spiritual life: recollection, detachment, and spiritual reading. They have been selected for discussion because of the essential role they play in the attainment of satisfactory meditation.

It was noted in an earlier chapter that success at meditation is dependent, to a large degree, upon factors which lie outside the limits of the formal meditation period. Many would find meditation less a problem if they were to concentrate on eradicating from their lives those elements which, while seemingly foreign to meditation, hinder in a very positive way the full development of mental prayer. And, while all the virtues of the spiritual life will assist in facilitating meditation, there are some which, because of their intrinsic relationship to prayer, are indispensable to successful conversation with Christ. The subject matter of this section—recollection, detachment, and spiritual reading—represents a summary of those exterior factors which bear such strong influence upon meditation.[1]

It would be impossible in these short chapters to present an adequate description of the nature and function of these practices; entire volumes have been consumed in evaluating these topics. Our sole intent, then will be to correlate their importance to meditation, and offer some general suggestions for implementing their development in our personal lives. We will begin with recollection. . . .

A venerable maxim, attributed to Blessed Claude de la Columbiere states: "He prays very little who prays only when he is on his knees." We might go one step further and claim: "He prays very *poorly* who prays only when he is on his knees." For the degree of contact with Christ during meditation is proportionate to the amount of contact we maintain with Him throughout the day. If one remains close to Our Lord during his entire day, through the use of aspirations and short prayers, he will experience little difficulty in continuing this relationship during his meditation. But if, on the

---

[1] The material discussed in these chapters falls under the category of general (or remote) preparation for prayer. In a strictly logical sequence, this would have been treated in Chapter 5; but in order to launch immediately into our description of Teresian meditation, it was postponed until this point.

other hand, he works out his daily routine in an atmosphere devoid of Christ, he will encounter an initial struggle in establishing contact with Our Lord. We remain close to Christ in our daily activities so that we may draw closer to Him in our meditation.

St. Teresa in her exposition on the intimate nature of mental prayer postulates this practice of recollection (or, as it is better known, the presence of God) as an essential preparatory factor for meditation:

> We must cast aside everything else, they say, in order to approach God inwardly and we must retire within ourselves even during our ordinary occupations. If I can recall the companionship which I have within my soul for as much as a moment, that is a great utility.[2]

> If she can, let her practice recollection many times daily; if not, let her do it occasionally. As she grows accustomed to it, she will feel its benefits, either sooner or later. Once the Lord has granted it to her, she would not exchange it for any treasure.[3]

One of St. Teresa's modern commentators refers to the position of importance given to habitual recollection in her treatise:

> In her teaching on mental prayer, very rarely does St. Teresa distinguish between the time that is especially set aside for it, and the rest of the day. To the presence of God, abiding and always acting in us, there must correspond a striving for intimacy as constant as possible. The prayer of recollection must overflow progressively into all of our life.[4]

---

[2] St. Teresa, *Way of Perfection,* xxix.

[3] *Ibid.*

[4] P. Marie-Eugene, O.C.D., *I Want to See God,* trans. Sr. M. Verda Clare, C.S.C. (Chicago: Fides Publishers Association, 1953), p. 202.

But according to the mind of Teresa, the prayer of recollection must extend over the entire day and penetrate the whole of the life.[5]

The precise function of recollection in relation to meditation is presented in terse summary by another of St. Teresa's Carmelite commentators:

The positive element (of preparation for mental prayer) is the exercise of the presence of God, which we endeavor to make continuous as far as possible. Fidelity to this practice develops in us increasing facility in speaking with God and greater ease in establishing intimate contact with Him.[6]

Granted, then, that habitual recollection is an invaluable asset to mental prayer; how does one achieve its practice? The most serviceable device for obtaining this goal is the utilization of small aspirations and prayers throughout the day. The emphasis here is on *short* and *interspersed.* Our continuous contact can be but a fleeting affair; not many of us have the time—or the mental equipment—which we can donate to prolonged periods of prayer throughout the day. The pressure of responsibilities and business requires that our habitual prayer be of brief duration. But this habitual prayer, albeit

---

[5] *Ibid.,* p. 207. St. Alphonsus would also be heard on this subject: ". . . it is an infallible rule that love is always increased by the presence of the object loved. This happens even among men. . . . How much more shall the love of a soul for God increase if it keeps Him before its eyes! for the more it converses with Him, the better it comprehends His beauty and amiableness. The morning and the evening meditation are not sufficient to keep the soul united with God . . . therefore after prayer it is necessary to preserve fervor by the presence of God, and by renewing our affections." *The True Spouse of Jesus Christ* (Brooklyn: Redemptorist Fathers, 1929), p. 499.

[6] Father Gabriel, *Little Catechism of Prayer*, p. 17.

"how well we can love Christ."

brief, must nevertheless be repeated constantly through the course of the day.

As in our formal meditation, our continuous contact with Christ embraces two elements: thought and will. We are to think of Christ, but—more important—we are to make an affective response to Him. The basic value of recollection consists not in how well we can think of Him, but rather, in how well we can love Him. Through our thought of Christ we are drawn to express our love for Him.

The constant remembrance of Christ may be facilitated by any one of three customary methods: external, imaginative, or intellectual presence of God.[7] The external practice consists in employing exterior objects as reminders of Our Lord's presence. A crucifix, holy picture, etc. can be a tangible means for awakening us to the nearness of Christ. The imaginative presence relies on a mental depicting of Our Lord in a position close to us. Finally, intellectual recollection effects a remembrance of God's presence by means of some doctrine of faith: a consideration of the Trinity's presence in our souls, God's protective Providence, etc.

But whichever of these means we adopt to bring the presence of God to our minds, we are still obliged to cement our contact with Christ through the function of the will expressed in acts of love. St. Francis de Sales gives us the proper perspective in these phrases:

> Make . . . frequent aspirations to God by short but ardent motions of your heart; admire His beauty; implore His assistance; cast yourself in spirit at the foot of the cross; adore

[7] Cf. *Ibid.*, pp. 41-44.

His goodness; converse with Him frequently on the affairs
of your salvation; present your soul to Him a thousand times
a day . . . and make a thousand different motions of your
heart, to enkindle and excite within yourself a passionate
and tender affection for your Divine Spouse.[8]

This advertance to God can be employed continually
throughout our day despite the preoccupations of our
state in life. St. Alphonsus comments:

The first method consists in frequently raising the heart to
God, by short but fervent ejaculations, or loving affections
towards God present within us. These may be practiced in
all places and in all times, in walking, at work, at meals, and
at recreation. These affections may be acts of election, of
desire, of resignation, of oblation, of love, of renunciation,
of thanksgiving, of petition, of humiliation, of confidence,
and the like. In whatever occupation you find yourself, you
can very easily turn to God from time to time . . .[9]

An admonition is in order here: the struggle to remain recollected admits varying degrees of success, and
is a process of gradual development; consequently, the
effort to attain recollection should be free from stress
and tension. If our labor to remain near Christ should
upset and distract us, it will have defeated its very purpose. St. Alphonsus notes:

And it is necessary, first, to know that to remain always before God, with the mind always fixed on Him, is the happy
lot of the saints; but in the present state it is morally impossible to keep the presence of God without interruption.
Hence, we should endeavor to practice it to the best of our

[8] St. Francis de Sales, *Introduction to a Devout Life,* II, 13.
[9] St. Alphonsus, *The True Spouse of Jesus Christ,* p. 508.

ability, not with a solicitous inquietude and indiscreet effort of the mind, but with sweetness and tranquility.[10]

A closer union with Christ can be obtained, though, by a continuous, tranquil, gradual effort. The rather fantastic account of Father William Doyle's daily total of aspirations comes to mind. By dint of determined effort he raised the daily count of his aspirational prayer to a staggering one-hundred thousand.[11] Much speculation has been offered as to the precise system of enumeration he employed; but no matter which method he did employ (and surely it was not our conventional system) the fact remains that he labored diligently and successfully to increase the total of his aspirations. While we cannot hope to emulate the sum of Father Doyle's prayers, we can imitate his vigorous efforts—and some portion of his success will be ours.

The practice of recollection, therefore, has as its object the attainment of a more facile entry into our meditation. It will obviate the loss of valuable time expended in an attempt to establish contact with Christ; and it will make the realization of this contact more certain. But, after all, it was Our Lord Himself who commanded us to utilize this procedure:

You ought always to pray.[12]   *Luke 18, 1*

---

[10] *Ibid.*

[11] Cf. Alfred O'Rahilly, *Father William Doyle, S.J.* (New York: Longmans Green, 1928), pp. 211 ff. Father "Willie" Doyle notes: "Jesus wants me to work with might and main to acquire the interior union so that not for one moment would I forget His presence within me." (p. 217) Also cf. pp. 452, 459, and 466 for an account of his heroic struggle in this exercise.

[12] Luke, 18, 1.

And St. Paul commented on it:

Pray without ceasing.[13]

The more recollection we maintain outside the time of meditation, the better mental prayer we will experience; and the less recollection we have, the less success will be ours at meditation. This is a ruthless ratio—but one that is constantly verified.

[13] 1 Thess., 5, 7.

18

DETACHMENT

RECOLLECTION is the positive preparation for meditation; the subject matter of the present chapter embraces the negative preparatory factors for prayer—mortification and humility, grouped under the generic title, detachment.

Meditation is primarily an exercise of love in which we express our affection and loyalty to Christ. Those factors in life which enhance the love of Christ in our souls facilitate mental prayer; and those factors which diminish our love for Christ erect grave obstacles to meditation. The principal hindrances to our love for Christ are two—external objects, to which we donate some of the affection due to Christ; and our own selves *on health* (self-love), to which we assign a greater or lesser amount of our interest and concern. We can combat the first source of misplaced love—exterior objects—through mortification, and the second source—self-love—through humility of heart. We will treat of them in that order, mortification and then humility.

The term "mortification" is derived from an old Latin word denoting a process of killing something or someone. In its religious sense, mortification expresses the procedure of killing those affections which hinder our love for Christ. While mortification is, in its basic outlines, a negative thing, it has an entirely positive goal and objective—the enjoyment of a greater love for Christ.

All who would save their souls are obliged to practice some amount of mortification—at least that degree which extirpates loves and desires forbidden under penalty of mortal sin. Those who would live a more holy life intensify their practice of mortification in an endeavor to eradicate venial sin, and finally even imperfections. All of this is standard theological doctrine, and we would not tarry here in the present discussion. Our treatment of mortification is concerned only with its relationship to meditation (and a very close relationship it does have).

Meditation is an act of love for Christ; and if He is the principal love of our life, our meditations will be executed with greater success and ease. But if we enter into meditation encumbered with a variety of loves and affections opposed to Christ, our prayer would suffer accordingly. Mortification, therefore, struggles to root out these rebellious affections.

The human heart is capable of latching its affections onto a variety of animate and inanimate objects; it is prodigal of its love. This dissipation of love-energy hinders it from loving any one thing completely. Christ Himself firmly proclaimed:

Jesus said to love God with all your heart, mind, soul and strength and your neighbor as yourself.
Jesus said love one Detachment *another as* 131 *I have loved you.*

No man can serve two masters; for either he will hate the one and love the other, or else he will be loyal to one and despise the other.[1]

Love to be perfect must be exclusive. The more we try to divide our love, the less capable we will be of loving any one thing perfectly. This is verified in our relations with God: we cannot hope to share our love for Him with any creature—animate or inanimate—if we desire to love Him fully. St. John of the Cross lucidly discusses this question:

It is for this reason that we say of this state that it is the making of two wills into one—namely, into the will of God, which will of God is likewise the will of the soul. For if this soul desired any imperfection that God wills not, there would not be made one will of God, since the soul would have a will for that which God had not . . . These habitual imperfections are, for example, a common custom of much speaking, or some attachment which we never wish entirely to conquer—such as that to a person, a garment, a book, a cell, a particular kind of food, tittle tattle, fancies for tasting, knowing or hearing certain things, and such like. Any one of these imperfections, if the soul has become attached and habituated to it, is of as great harm to its growth and progress in virtue as though it were to fall daily into many other imperfections and casual venial sins.[2]

Habitual affection for creatures detracts from our love for God. Yes, but why? St. John also answers that question:

. . . from the very fact that the soul becomes affectioned to a thing which comes under the head of creature, that the more

---

[1] Luke, 16, 13.
[2] St. John of the Cross, *Ascent of Mount Carmel*, I, ch. 11, 3 and 4.

desire for that thing fills the soul, the less capacity has the soul for God; inasmuch as two contraries, according to the philosophers, cannot co-exist in one person; and further, since . . . affection for God and affection for creatures are contraries, and thus there cannot be contained within one will affection for creatures and affection for God.[3]

St. John enunciates an ancient physical axiom: two contraries cannot exist in the same subject at the same time. This physical axiom is verified also in the psychological realm: two equal loves cannot exist in one person at the same time. "We love the one or hate the other," says Christ.

The Doctor of Carmel supplies the remedy for this deficiency in our love for God:

. . . to love is to labor to detach and strip itself for God's sake of all that is not God.[4]

This is the reason underlying our insistence upon a generous spirit of mortification in preparation for meditation. By mortifying our sense appetite we eradicate the obstacles to a full friendship with Christ. Consequently, St. Teresa is adamant in her assertion of the necessity of mortification for successful mental prayer:

For this and for many reasons, in writing of the first kind of prayer . . . I pointed out that it is most important for souls, when they begin to practice prayer, to start by detaching themselves from every kind of pleasure, and to enter upon

---

[3] *Ibid.*, ch. 6, 1.

[4] *Ibid.*, II, ch. 5, 7. For a clear exposition of St. John of the Cross' doctrine of detachment cf. Father Gabriel of St. Mary Magdalene, O.C.D., *St. John of the Cross, Doctor of Divine Love and Contemplation* (Cork: Mercier Press, 1946), pp. 21-43.

their prayer with one sole determination, to help Christ bear His cross.[5]

... for, you know, if prayer is to be genuine it must be re-enforced with these things—prayer cannot be accompanied by self-indulgence.[6]

It would be beyond the scope of the present discussion to present a detailed outline of the various exercises of mortification. However, a few general norms might be offered. Mortification should be undertaken with a realistic view of its positive function in the spiritual life; and the more one develops in the love of God, the more generosity he will evidence in self-denial.[7] But that is not to infer that a program of mortification should be deferred until one has attained a high degree of love for God. Mortification and love go hand-in-hand; they increase simultaneously and reciprocally.

Self-denial must be a generous, vigorous effort. While it is better to begin with smaller practices, these should grow into more heroic ones; mortification is a progressive adventure. A word of caution must be inserted about excessive physical penances, and those which are beyond our physical or psychological strength. St. John of the Cross cautions us to proceed with "order and discretion"

---

[5] St. Teresa, *Life*, xv.

[6] St. Teresa, *Way of Perfection*, iv.

[7] St. John of the Cross, *Ascent of Mount Carmel*, I, ch. 14, 2: "For, in order to conquer all the desires and to deny itself the pleasures which it has in everything, and for which its love and affection are wont to enkindle the will that it may enjoy them, it would be necessary to experience another and a greater enkindling by another and a better love, which is that of its Spouse; to the end that, having its pleasure set upon Him and deriving from Him its strength, it should have courage and constancy to deny itself all other things with ease."

in our self-denial.[8] It would be advisable for beginners in the spiritual life to limit themselves entirely to the less physical mortifications.

Our exercise of mortification, though, should be *generous* and *constant*. These two adjectives summarize the doctrine of mortification: a generous eradication of loves detrimental to Christ, and a constant effort in self-denial. With a constant, generous mortification, we will make surer progress in the ways of meditation.

Humility

Love of creatures, therefore, will hinder our love for Christ—if this be so of those external objects mentioned above, it is even more true of that most absorbing creature, one's own self. To extinguish this subtle love of self, St. Teresa insists on the virtue of humility. In fact, she postulates humility as an essential prerequisite for mental prayer:

> . . . the entire foundation of prayer must be established in humility.[9]

In writing of the state of mind opposed to humility (pride and undue concern for one's reputation), St. Teresa vigorously states:

> I repeat this: however slight may be our concern for our reputation, the result of it will be as bad as when we play a wrong note, or make a mistake in time, in playing the organ —the whole passage will become discordant. Such concern is

---

[8] *Ibid.*, ch. 12, 7. Cf. also St. Francis de Sales, *Introduction to a Devout Life*, III, 23.

[9] St. Teresa, *Life*, xxii.

Healthy self-love is good? am a child of God.

Unhealthy self-love Detachment *is not good,* 135 *because it is not based on truth. We have to distinguish between healthy self-love and un- healthy self-love.*

a thing which harms the soul whenever it occurs; but in the life of prayer it is pestilential.[10]

"The foundation of prayer," "In the life of prayer it is pestilential"—these are strong phrases. But St. Teresa is an expert in the science of prayer, and knows whereof she speaks. She was aware of the dangers involved in an excessive preoccupation with self. She knew, in fact, that meditation without an attendant humility is fraught with obstacles. After all, in this she is merely paraphrasing the doctrine of sacred scripture:

> God resists the proud and gives grace to the humble.[11]
>
> He has had regard to the prayer of the humble.[12]
>
> The prayer of him that humbleth himself shall pierce the clouds.[13]

Only through an understanding of humility's nature and function can one appreciate the significance of these statements. Humility, by way of definition, is a virtue which gives us a realistic understanding of our position in the universe through an evaluation of our inherent poverty. In other words, humility strikes a lethal blow at self-love by disengaging us from our native fascination with our own excellence. Pride tends to focus one's affective powers inward upon himself; humility creates a dissatisfaction with self and turns the soul's love outward upon God.

St. Teresa has given the most serviceable approach to

[10] *Ibid.*, xxxi.
[11] James, 4, 6.
[12] Psalm 101, 18.
[13] Ecclus., 25, 21.

Humility is Truth.

Jesus said I am "the Truth, the Way, the Life
136   Conversation with Christ
Jesus also said I am meek and humble

this rather mysterious virtue in her now famous statement:

> I was wondering once why Our Lord so dearly loved this virtue of humility; and all of a sudden . . . the following reason came into my mind: that it is because God is sovereign truth and to be humble is to walk in truth, for it is absolutely true to say that we have no good thing in ourselves, but only misery and nothingness; and anyone who fails to understand this is walking in falsehood. He who best understands this is most pleasing to sovereign truth because he is walking in truth.[14]

There it is: humility is *truth.* That single word—truth—summarizes the nature and function of humility. It is a studied attempt to realize our own position in relation to God; and when the results of this study have been assessed, the soul finds self-love almost impossible.

What will the truth demonstrate to us? It will clearly show us that we are purely contingent creatures, dependent in every respect upon God. As Christ said: "Without Me you can do nothing." [15] These words of Our Lord are all inclusive: we can perform nothing in a natural or supernatural sphere without the immediate support of God [16]—the only exception, the single thing of which we ourselves are capable is *sin.*[17] Thus, St. Paul summarizes the situation:

[14] St. Teresa, *Interior Castle*, VI, x.

[15] John. 15, 5.

[16] "If any man think himself to be something, whereas he is nothing, he deceiveth himself." Gal., 6.3.

[17] For a precise, theological explanation of this point cf. William Most, *Mary in Our Life* (New York: Kenedy, 1953), p. 103.

Or what hast thou that thou has not received? And if thou hast received it, why dost thou boast as if thou hast not received it? [18]

This appreciation of our utter dependence upon God represents the first of two mental attitudes necessary for humility; the second attitude consists in a recognition of our inferiority in relation to our fellow-men. St. Paul reminds us:

assume

In humility let each esteem others better than themselves. [19]
ourselves

an attitude

Is this possible? In all truth and fairness, we do recognize that we are in a better spiritual position than many other people. Are we asked to develop an unreasonable, unrealistic, untrue evaluation of our relative position to others?—assuredly not, for humility is truth. St. Thomas Aquinas solves this apparently contradictory situation. He maintains that we may distinguish two separate elements in a human being—that which is of God, and that which we have of ourselves (namely, sin). [20] By comparing that which we have of ourselves (sin) with that which is from God in others (all their qualities, save sin), we may justly conclude that we are inferior to each person in the world. [21]

We shouldn't compare

We are using selective truth, not the whole truth!

[18] 1 Cor., 4, 7.

[19] Phil., 2, 3.

[20] "In man two things may be considered: what is of God and what there is of man. Of man there is whatever points to defect; but of God, all that makes for salvation and perfection." St. Thomas Aquinas, *Summa Theologica*, II-II, q. 161, a. 3.

[21] "We ought to revere God not only in Himself, but we ought also to revere what is of Him in all persons; but not with the same degree of reverence that we give to God." *Ibid.*

This habitual (attitude) of judging ourselves inferior in relation to God and our fellow-men will engender in us the virtue of humility.[22] And when we have acquired humility of heart we have destroyed self-love, one more obstacle to our love for God—in fact, the most persistent, subtle of all obstacles.

The two virtues treated here—mortification and humility—might at first blush appear strange bed-fellows for a joint discussion. However, they both possess the same objective: destruction of affection for creatures— one attacking love for exterior creatures, the other stifling love for that interior creature, self. Consequently, St. Teresa combines these two virtues in her treatise on prayer:

> It is here that true humility can enter, for this virtue and that of detachment from self, I think, always go together. They are two sisters, who are inseparable.[23]

If we generously and courageously detach ourselves from all but Christ, we will experience new ease in engaging Our Lord in conversation. There will be no misplaced affection to hinder the union of the soul with Christ. Our Lord is a true lover—He will allow no opponent. Or, as the author of the *Imitation* has poignantly pleaded:

> We must leave what is beloved for the sake of the Beloved;

---

[22] For an excellent, detailed discussion of this virtue cf. Cajetan da Bergamo, *Humility of Heart,* trans. Vaughn (Westminster: Newman Press, 1944). Also cf. Father Canice, O.F.M. Cap., *Humility the Foundation of the Spiritual Life* (Westminster: Newman, 1951).

[23] St. Teresa, *Way of Perfection*, x.

for Jesus will be loved alone and above all things . . . The nature of thy Beloved is such that He will not admit of a rival; but He will have thy heart for Himself alone, and sit as a King upon His own throne.[24]

---

[24] *Imitation of Christ*, Bk. II, ch. 7.

CHAPTER

19

SPIRITUAL READING

"TELL ME WHAT YOU READ," runs an old saw, "and I will tell you what you are." As trite as the phrase may be, it contains a valid, incontestable truth: reading ✦ *influence* shapes our minds and lives in a manner almost beyond ✦ realization. One's reading matter is an infallible gauge ✦ of his intellectual, moral and religious habits of mind. ✦ Consequently, spiritual writers of the centuries have assigned a significant position to spiritual reading in the full development of one's spiritual life. And, of more importance for us in the present discussion, spiritual reading exercises a definite influence upon our meditation.

St. Teresa stresses the value of learning and spiritual education for the practice of mental prayer:

> Other persons will profit in this way, especially if they are learned; for learning, I think, is a priceless help in this exercise, if humility goes with it. Only a few days ago I observed that this was so in certain learned men, who began but a short while since and have made great progress; and

this gives me great longings that many more learned men should become spiritual . . .[1]

We pointed out previously the advantageous results that accrue to an individual's meditation from a supply of knowledge about the subject and scene selected for daily prayer. One experiences greater ease in handling the meditation material when he possesses a fuller comprehension of it. This instruction in spiritual issues is, in ordinary circumstances, obtained through good spiritual reading. The Gospels, lives of Christ, and commentaries on scripture furnish us with background material for prayer. Books of spiritual doctrine, works on practical spirituality, and biographies present us with proper attitudes of mind to be employed in our conversation with Christ.

Meditation is not solely an emotional, affective approach to Christ; it is, rather, a mature, intelligent act of friendship for Our Lord. This intelligent companionship demands, of necessity, some amount of education in spiritual values; and this education is derived principally through spiritual reading. St. Teresa notes in her autobiography the beneficial results that reading produced in her own prayer life.[2] She sums up the matter by stating:

It seemed to me, in these early stages of which I am speaking, that, provided I had books and could be alone, there was no risk of my being deprived of that great blessing . . .[3]

[1] St. Teresa, *Life*, xii.
[2] Cf. *Ibid.*, iv.
[3] *Ibid.*

All of this represents the direct effects of spiritual reading upon the actual meditation period. Spiritual reading also bears an indirect influence upon mental prayer, and this is perhaps of even greater importance than the direct influence. Through the direct influence we master spiritual truths and facts to employ at prayer; through the indirect influence of reading we create a climate in which it becomes increasingly easier to conduct our conversation with Christ. We live in a world devoid, in great part, of a Christian spirit, in an atmosphere and culture estranged from God. Living in such a non-theological environment makes it difficult for us to remain in contact with the person of Christ and the true purpose of life itself. We must, if we are to remain realistically attached to Christ, combat this atmosphere and surround ourselves with a new one. Constant spiritual reading fills our minds with Christ and His doctrine —it creates this new climate for us.

In former ages, spiritual reading was not as essential for one's prayer life. People lived in a Christian world and culture which was reflected in their laws, customs, amusements, and their very outlook on life. This situation has radically altered in the last two hundred years, and men must now compensate for this deficit through other media, principally reading. And as the de-Christianization of our world continues, the necessity for spiritual reading simultaneously increases.[4] We stand

---

[4] For an intelligent, articulate discussion of the correlation between meditation and spiritual reading cf. Eugene Boylan, O.Cist., *This Tremendous Lover* (Westminster: Newman, 1947), pp. 99-112. Father Boylan remarks: "To our mind (spiritual reading), ranks equally with mental prayer and the other exercises of devotion in importance, and

in need of something to bridge the gap between our
pagan surroundings and our conversation with Christ—
spiritual reading fills this need.

There is today in our country an alarming decline in
general reading of all types. It has been estimated that
in 1955 an astonishing forty-eight percent of the American adult population read *no books at all,* and only
eighteen percent read from one to four books.[5] The
decline in reading is naturally reflected in religious
reading as well. And, while the lack of secular reading
will occasion a decrease in cultural life, the decline in
religious reading will have repercussions of a more serious nature—severe detriment to one's spiritual life. Any
serious attempt to better one's life spiritually should,
therefore, include the resolution to engage in more
spiritual reading.

If we confine our reading to non-Catholic books,
magazines and newspapers, we almost automatically
exclude ourselves from full development in our prayer
life. The maxims and philosophy of life expressed in
these avenues of communication slowly begin to seep
into our lives until eventually they occupy a ruling
position. We will not have surrounded ourselves with a
new climate; rather, the non-Catholic climate will have
engulfed us.

in fact, it is so closely connected with these other exercises, especially
the essential one of mental prayer, that without it—unless one finds
some substitute—there is no possibility of advancing in the spiritual
life; even perseverance therein is rendered very doubtful." (p. 101)

[5] These figures are quoted by David H. Russell, "We All Need to
Read," *Saturday Review of Literature,* XXXIX, No. 7 (Feb. 18, 1956),
p. 36.

Granted that books of immoral and non-Catholic content can harm us, but what of ordinary books containing no positive evil, are they similarly harmful? Not individually, but collectively, they are. The reading of individual books of a secular nature will not necessarily have undesirable effects upon us, but an <u>exclusive</u> diet of such reading definitely will. <u>The very fact that these books carefully exclude any reference to God or the purpose of life makes them suspect and dangerous. They present an unrealistic view of life—one without God.</u> The typical characters in a modern novel, for example, are enmeshed in a series of conflicts and crises (love, marriage, business, infidelity, frustration, etc.) <u>which find their expression and solution on a purely human, natural level. These characters are portrayed in such a manner that there is no reference to their relationship with God or their final destiny after death.</u> They work out their lives and careers on a single plane, the material one; but life is meant to be lived simultaneously on two planes, the natural *and* the supernatural. <u>Any attempt to portray people living on a single plane presents a picture which is incomplete, truncated, and false.</u> If we engage in much reading of this type, we gradually assimilate <u>this unrealistic philosophy of life</u>; and such a mental attitude fashions a hostile climate for meditation.

The criticism has been levied against spiritual reading that books of this type are difficult to digest. The complaint has been offered that many spiritual works are awkward translations of dull treatises intended for monks and nuns. These objections might have been valid fifty years ago, but are not today. Each year American Catholic publishers offer hundreds of new, interesting titles. Books of devotion, applied Catholicism, essays, and biography are presented in modern, readable, trenchant language. No convincing excuse could be offered by our modern, educated American for excluding spiritual reading from his life.

Spiritual reading, then, is the third essential asset for meditation. Its immediate, direct result is to supply us with material and data for our conversation with Christ; its indirect, and vitally important, effect is to fashion a climate and environment which facilitates contact with Christ.

.   .   .

The subject matter of these three chapters has summarized the indispensable aids to meditation. Detachment (divided into mortification and humility) represents the negative preparation for prayer: a withdrawal from all that is not Christ. Recollection and spiritual reading constitute the positive preparation: an impregnation of the mind and heart with all that is Christ. If these practices be incorporated in our lives, the problems of meditation will be radically reduced.

VII

Progress
in Meditation

It is an immense advantage to
have enjoyed His friendship,
and to have felt the delights
with which He inundates souls
in the way of prayer.

—St. Teresa

CHAPTER

20

FACILITY IN MEDITATION

I T IS A COMMON PHENOMENON of life to attain greater facility in any occupation or skill through the investment of time and effort. Man naturally tends to grow more adept in the performance of a task as he learns its basic rules, and struggles to apply them. The young student beginning the study of a foreign language is forced to battle with a whole new world of verbs, nouns, and awkward constructions; but before long he acquires an adroitness in the language. Meditation follows this general pattern and admits of a gradual increase in the ease and poise with which it is performed.

Prescinding from any infusion of supernatural contemplation, we may state that everyone who diligently applies the norms and principles thus far outlined, may expect to acquire some natural facility and progress in meditation. The precise area in which this facility will be experienced is the conversation with Christ.

The entire structure of Teresian meditation is geared to the production of this conversation. The preliminary steps have as their sole purpose the introduction of the soul into a face-to-face meeting with Christ. Beginners will stand in need of a rather belabored journey through these introductory stages; and such a laborious procedure may result in only a relatively brief conversation— nevertheless, the meditation will have been eminently successful. Perhaps during a fifteen-minute period, one might consume the initial ten minutes in reading and reflection, and then find himself capable of sustaining but a five-minute conversation. All well and good; this is par for a beginner. But as the neophite begins to as- similate the principles of mental prayer, he will become more adroit in their application, and will gradually lengthen the period of conversation to six or seven, or even ten minutes duration. He has begun to acquire some of the natural facility at meditation.

The more one energetically devotes himself to mental prayer, the less need there will be to expend a great deal of time on the preparatory steps; in fact, a few minutes application of them might be all that is required. And finally, when meditation has become completely mas- tered, one may entirely exclude some of these prepara- tory exercises.

It is important to distinguish the essential from the non-essential in mental prayer; for when any single element in the Teresian outline of meditation is dis- covered to be no longer necessary for the realization of its essential goal (conversation with Our Lord), it should be omitted. The ability to delete certain steps in the outline may be habitual or occasional: one may find a particular step—say, the reading—quite necessary on one day, and entirely superfluous on another day. The reading prior to meditation and the attempt to place oneself in Christ's presence may be quite frequently omitted. The consideration (reflection) will be less often passed over; but then again at intervals it too might prove non-essential. It is quite conceivable that one who has become adept at mental prayer will be able to consume almost the entire period in conversation with Christ. The general principle to be applied here is: only those elements of meditation are to be employed which are immediately necessary for drawing one into conversation with Our Lord.

Many well-intentioned people feel they are remiss in the practice of meditation if they exclude one or another of its elements. For them St. Francis de Sales has a timely bit of advice:

> You must also know that it may sometimes happen that immediately after the preparation, you will feel your affections moved towards God. In this case . . . you must yield to the attraction, and cease to follow the method I have before given; for, although, generally speaking, consideration precedes affections and resolutions, yet when the Holy Ghost gives you the latter before the former, you must not then seek the former, since it is used for no other purpose than to excite the latter.[1]

A more homey, but nonetheless practical, meditation maxim maintains: "If you find the orange peeled, eat it." That is, if one is capable of entering into immediate contact with Christ, by no means should he delay on the other steps.

---

[1] St. Francis de Sales, *Introduction to a Devout Life*, II, 8.

The salient point to be remembered, though, is that one's mental prayer does improve, given time and effort. The danger is that the beginner at prayer may become so discouraged at the initial adjustment to mental prayer that he gives it up entirely as a bad job. St. Teresa, discussing the difficulties encountered as one undertakes meditation in earnest, warns:

> Nothing . . . can be learned without a little trouble, so do, for the love of God, look upon any care which you take about this well spent. I know that, with God's help, if you practice it for a year, or perhaps for only six months, you will be successful in attaining it. Think what a short time that is for acquiring so great a benefit. . . .[2]

Therefore, if we make a generous investment of time and energy, we will gradually acquire a definite ease and facility in mental prayer. Every human skill can be developed and perfected—meditation is no exception to this general fact of life.

---

[2] St. Teresa, *Way of Perfection*, xxix.

CHAPTER

21

ADVANCED MENTAL
PRAYER

OUR ENTIRE DISCUSSION of mental prayer thus far
has examined the fundamental aspects of meditation. A careful and deliberate effort has been made to exclude any investigation into the more advanced stages of
mental prayer. This was consonant with the general
theme of the book: to present a basic introduction to
meditation. However, the present chapter will deviate
slightly from this generic aim by offering a brief description of that stage of mental prayer which immediately
follows meditative prayer in the development of one's
spiritual life.

The question instantly comes to mind: why does an
introductory book on meditation pause to examine advanced prayer? The answer lies in the fact that any
manual of prayer should at least point out the paths
along which meditation will develop. For meditation is
not a static exercise of the spiritual life; it is, rather, a

dynamic procedure which leads the soul into new areas of intimacy with Christ.

In addition to charting the course along which mental prayer develops, the present chapter will serve to give some practical norms for those who discover that they have advanced beyond basic meditation. It is the contention of St. Teresa and St. John of the Cross that those who diligently engage in mental prayer will experience a rapid growth in their prayer life. If these fortunate souls be not advised of the characteristics and circumstances of advanced prayer, they might become confused and bewildered in their new state of spiritual maturity.

Mental prayer, as was said, is a progressive experience: it begins at simple meditation and evolves into mystical contemplation. The ultimate state of progress, mystical contemplation, is beyond the scope of this book. However, lying between basic meditation and mystical contemplation is a third stage which should be brought to the attention of all who generously undertake mental prayer. This third stage is a hybrid one: it possesses some characteristics of each of the other two states. From one vantage point it resembles meditation, and from another it bears similarities to pure contemplation. It is, however, a distinct phase of development in prayer. ✓

The nomenclature attributed to this species of mental prayer is confusing; spiritual authors seem to have vied with each other in coining new titles for it. The most common title is *acquired contemplation*—this is the traditional Carmelite term.[1] Others have employed different appellations: the prayer of simplicity, prayer of recollection, simple view of faith, active contemplation.[2] For the sake of clarity and conformity we will resist the temptation to create new terminology and employ the accepted term, acquired contemplation.[3]

The notion of acquired contemplation might be more easily communicated by a description of the soul's progress into this state. After some effort at meditation, one begins to obtain a natural facility at prayer as was discussed in the previous chapter. The need of belabored periods of consideration decreases rapidly, and the periods of actual conversation with Christ are protracted. In addition to enjoying an ease in conversing with Our Lord, one is also able to spend some time in a silent love of Christ. This represents the limits of the ordinary advancement in prayer. As the next phase develops the soul begins to experience difficulty in performing any considerations at all—in fact, ordinary medi-

---

[1] Cf. Fr. Gabriel of St. Mary Magdalene, O.C.D., *St. John of the Cross, Doctor of Divine Love*, pp. 108-202, and Joseph Guibert, S.J., *Theology of the Spiritual Life*, pp. 200-1.

The term 'acquired contemplation' is not in opposition to 'infused contemplation.' All contemplation—even the imperfect type—is to some extent infused. The significance of the term 'acquired' lies in the fact that those who enjoy this type of prayer must still elicit positive acts of intellect and will.

[2] Adolphe Tanquerey, *The Spiritual Life* (Tournai: Society of St. John, 1930), p. 637.

[3] Supernatural contemplation, in general, is defined as "a simple gaze on truth under the influence of love." (Cf. Fr. M. Eugene, *I Want to See God*, pp. 458 and 463.) Acquired contemplation is that species which is not completely passive and demands the soul's cooperation and concomitant activity.

tation becomes well-nigh impossible. However, the soul remains very much in the presence of God and silently expresses its affection for Him. Concomitant with these experiences, the soul begins to grow aware of an increasing aridity—there is little sensible consolation in this new contact with Christ; it is an arid attention to Our Lord.

This descriptive portrait of acquired contemplation demonstrates the principal characteristics of the state. By way of definition we may say that acquired contemplation is a stage of development in mental prayer in which meditative reflections are unnecessary and impossible, but in which the soul remains in arid contact with God.[4]

St. John of the Cross lucidly describes the development into acquired contemplation in his *Living Flame of Love*. Let us quote the Doctor of the Church at some length so that he may present his thought completely:

> And in order that we may better understand the characteristics of beginners, we must know that the state and exercise of beginners is one of meditation and of the making of discursive exercises and acts with the imagination. In this state it is necessary for the soul to be given material for meditation and reasoning, and it is well for it to make interior acts on its own account, and even in spiritual things to take advantage of the sweetness and pleasure which come from sense; for, if the desire is fed with pleasure in spiritual things, it becomes detached from pleasure in sensual things and wearies of things of the world. But when to some extent

---

[4] The definition offered is a practical, psychological one rather than an ontological explanation of the nature of acquired contemplation. It is our purpose here to present a working definition.

the desire has been fed, and in some sense habituated to spiritual things, and has acquired some fortitude and constancy, God then begins, as they say, to wean the soul and bring it into the state of contemplation, which in some persons is wont to happen very quickly, especially in religious, because these, having renounced things of the world, quickly attune their sense and desire to God, and their exercises become spiritual through God's works in them; this happens when the discursive acts and the meditation of the soul itself cease, and the first fervors and sweetness of sense cease likewise, so that the soul cannot meditate as before, or find any help in the senses; for the senses remain in a state of aridity, inasmuch as their treasure is transformed into spirit, and no longer falls within the capacity of sense. And, as all the operations which the soul can perform on its own account naturally depend upon sense only, it follows that God is the agent in this state and the soul is the recipient; for the soul behaves only as one that receives and as one in whom these things are being wrought; and God is One that gives and acts and as One that works these things in the soul, giving it spiritual blessings in contemplation, which is divine love and knowledge in one—that is, a loving knowledge, wherein the soul has not to use its natural acts and meditations, for it can no longer enter into them as before.[5]

St. John is not speaking here of pure (mystic) contemplation in which God is the sole agent; rather, he is describing acquired contemplation in which the individual must cooperate with God's action. The soul's operation is both negative and positive. In the negative sphere St. John of the Cross counsels:

It follows that at this time the soul must be led in a way entirely contrary to the way wherein it was led at first. If formerly it was given material for meditation, this material

---

[5] St. John of the Cross, *Living Flame of Love*, Stanza III, 32.

must now be taken from it and it must not meditate; for, as I say it will be unable to do so even though it would, and instead of becoming recollected, it will become distracted.[6]

In addition to this cessation of discursive meditation, St. John demands a detachment from sensible consolation:

And if formerly it sought sweetness and love and fervor, and found it, now it must neither seek it nor desire it, for not only will it be unable to find it through its own diligence, but it will rather find aridity, for it turns from the quiet and peaceful blessings which were secretly given to its spirit, to the work that it desires to do with sense; and thus it will lose the one and not obtain the other, since no blessings are now given to it by means of sense as they were formerly.[7]

And he summarizes both these negative procedures:

Wherefore in this state the soul must never have meditation imposed upon it, nor must it perform any acts, nor strive after sweetness or fervor; for this would be to set an obstacle in the way of the principal agent, who, as I say, is God.[8]

On the positive side, the Doctor of Carmel requires from the soul engaged in acquired contemplation a general, loving attention to God:

On its part let (the soul) simply, lovingly fix its attention upon God, without specific acts. Let it occupy itself . . . in loving attention, quite simply, as one who opens his eyes and fixes them upon a beloved object.[9]

---

[6] *Ibid.*
[7] *Ibid.*
[8] *Ibid.*
[9] *Ibid.*

The elevation to a new stage of mental prayer is a critical event in one's spiritual life. One would not wish to thrust himself precipitously into this new area if God had not called him there; nor should he tarry on simple meditative prayer when God has advanced him to a higher stage. To struggle along with a form of prayer beyond which it has now advanced would cause serious maladjustment in the soul's approach to God: frustrations, unrest, and discouragement would encumber the soul. On the other hand, it is equally disadvantageous to attempt the exercise of acquired contemplation previous to the invitation from God: one would be wasting his time in aimless reveries. The decision as to whether or not one is capable of acquired contemplation is most important. Therefore, St. John of the Cross describes three infallible signs whereby the soul at prayer (or more properly, his director) may ascertain the advisability of commencing the exercise of acquired contemplation.[10] These three criteria exclude the possibility that the soul's

---

[10] St. John of the Cross describes these three criteria in two separate places in his works—in the *Ascent of Mount Carmel*, II, 13; and in *Dark Night of the Soul*, I, 9. In the *Ascent* he writes: "In order that there may be no confusion in this instruction it will be meet in this chapter to explain at what time and season it behoves the spiritual person to lay aside the task of discursive meditation as carried on through the imaginations and forms and figures above mentioned, in order that he may lay them aside neither sooner or later than when the Spirit bids him; for, although it is meet for him to lay them aside at the proper time in order that he may journey to God and not be hindered by them it is no less needful for him not to lay aside the said imaginative meditation before the proper time lest he should turn backward. . . . We shall therefore here give certain signs and examples which the spiritual person will find in himself, whereby he may know if it is meet for him to lay them aside or not at this season."

arid attention to Christ may have arisen from any source except the action of God.

To insure the validity of this new stage of prayer St. John posits the first essential requirement:

> The first sign is his realization that he can no longer meditate or reason with his imagination, neither can (he) take pleasure therein as he was wont to do aforetime; he rather finds aridity in that which aforetime was wont to attract his senses and to bring him sweetness.[11]

The inability to meditate is of itself not a conclusive indication that one has advanced to acquired contemplation; for arid prayer may arise from a variety of other causes. Hence we must move on to the second sign:

> The second sign is a realization that he has no desire to fix his meditation or sense upon other particular objects, exterior or interior. I do not mean that the imagination neither comes nor goes (for it is wont to move freely even at times of great recollection), but that the soul has no pleasure in fixing it of set purpose upon other objects.[12]

This sign excludes the possibility that any affection for sin or creatures may be the cause of one's inability to meditate. The soul experiences a lack of consolation from both God and creatures. St. John comments elsewhere: ". . . the soul finds no pleasure or consolation in the things of God, it also fails to find it in anything created." [13]

---

[11] St. John of the Cross, *Ascent of Mount Carmel*, II, 13.

[12] *Ibid.*

[13] St. John of the Cross, *Dark Night*, 9, 2. Joined to this sign is the soul's hesitating fear that it is not serving God faithfully. St. John notes: ". . . ordinarily the memory is centered on God with painful care and solicitude, thinking that it is not serving God, but is back-

These are the two negative criteria. St. John's third sign is a positive one:

> The third and surest sign is that the soul takes pleasure in being alone, and waits with loving attentiveness upon God, without making any particular meditation, in inward peace and quietness and rest, and without acts and exercises of the faculties—memory, understanding, and will—at least, without discursive acts, that is, without passing from one thing to another; the soul is alone, with an attentiveness and a knowledge, general and loving, as we said, but without any particular understanding, and adverting not to what it is contemplating.[14]

This affectionate attentiveness to God is the keynote of acquired contemplation. If this sign, plus the other two, be present one may safely conclude that God is calling him to the practice of acquired contemplation. St. John, however, stresses that all three signs must be simultaneously present:

> These three signs, at least, the spiritual person must see in himself, all together, before he can venture with security to abandon the state of meditation and sense, and to enter that of contemplation and spirit.[15]

Presuming that our fervent soul has definitely advanced to acquired contemplation, what is to be his manner of operation in this state? First of all, there

---

sliding because it finds itself without sweetness in the things of God. And in such a case it is evident that this lack of sweetness and this aridity come not from weakness and lukewarmness; for it is the nature of lukewarmness not to care greatly or to have any inward solicitude for the things of God." (*Dark Night*, I, 9, 3)

[14] St. John of the Cross, *Ascent*, II, 14, 4.

[15] *Ibid.*, 5.

✓ should be no violent effort to resume methodic meditation. Ordinary meditation is now too elementary for the
soul; and any attempt to renew it would conflict with
God's action. Secondly, the soul is to direct a general,
loving attention to God. The soul's activity here is mini-
mal, but it is critical. If one be negligent in retaining his
attention upon God, there is danger that mere reverie
will take over. The soul is not to make precise reflections, but instead to remain in God's company and be
content with a loving awareness of His presence. It is
possible that distractions may still be experienced in this
stage of prayer, and the soul must make the same determined efforts to eradicate them. Then, too, one must
prepare for mental prayer by reading and other introductory acts—even though these need not be of such an
extensive nature as is required in the case of beginners.[16]

The form of prayer described here is an initial contemplation. Therefore, the soul develops gradually by
experiencing the new manner of prayer occasionally for
short periods of time before entering completely into it.
Also, one who has been enjoying acquired contemplation for some time may be compelled to resume ordinary
meditation once again for specified periods. St. John
of the Cross teaches:

> With regard to what has been said, there might be raised
> one question—if progressives . . . must never again, because
> of this that they are beginning to experience, return to the
> way of meditation and argument and natural forms. To this

---

[16] For a series of precise directives for souls in the state of acquired
contemplation cf. Fr. Marie-Eugene, O.C.D., *I Am a Daughter of the
Church,* trans. Sr. M. Verda Clare, C.S.C. (Chicago: Fides Publishers,
1955), pp. 86-93.

the answer is that it is not to be understood that such as are beginning to experience this loving knowledge must never again, as a general rule, try to return to meditation; for when they are first gaining in proficiency, the habit of contemplation is not yet so perfect that whensoever they wish they can give themselves to the act thereof, nor, in the same way, have they reached a point so far beyond meditation that they cannot occasionally meditate and reason in a natural way, as they were wont, using the figures and the steps that they were wont to use, and finding something new in them.[17]

The call to acquired contemplation does not infer that the soul is never to meditate again in the conventional manner. It should simply follow the action of God in mental prayer: if ordinary meditation is possible, it should be employed; but if God seems to be leading one into acquired contemplation, he should faithfully adjust himself to that mode of prayer. It seems that God usually introduces one into acquired contemplation for brief periods before He establishes the soul permanently in that state.[18]

All of this might appear quite confusing to the beginner at meditation. However, the things discussed in this chapter are not the concern of beginners. They have been mentioned so that one may have some general notion of God's plan of development in mental prayer.[19] When the moment of acquired contemplation

---

[17] St. John of the Cross, *Ascent*, II, 15, 1.

[18] Gabriel of St. Mary Magdalen, O.C.D., *St. John of the Cross*, p. 167.

[19] Note once again St. John's doctrine that acquired contemplation is obtained rather quickly by those who are diligent in the exercise of recollection and mortification: "To recollected persons this commonly happens sooner after their beginnings than to others, inasmuch as they are freer from occasions of backsliding, and their desires turn more

arrives in one's life he should consult a competent director.[20] The matters herein discussed will serve to present a general picture of what is to be expected.

The consoling element in the consideration of advanced mental prayer is that God reciprocates our friendship for Him with an invitation to greater intimacy at prayer. God is good—the more we seek Him out, the closer He will draw us to Himself.

---

quickly from the things of the world, which is what is needful if they are to begin to enter this blessed night of sense. Ordinarily no great time passes after their beginning before they begin to enter this night of sense; and the great majority of them do in fact enter it, for they will generally be seen to fall into these aridities." (*Dark Night*, I, 8, 4.)

[20] The need of personal direction throughout the advanced stages of mental prayer is essential. Each soul develops along different lines according to his temperament and dispositions. (Cf. Marie-Eugene, *I Want to See God*, 472-4.) Therefore, intelligent direction by a skilled priest is necessary to apply the general principles of advanced prayer to the particular case at hand.

VIII

The Royal Highway

In the way of mental prayer you proceed by a royal highway, since the King of Heaven has traced it out for you.

—St. Teresa

22

ST. TERESA'S ROYAL
HIGHWAY

IN A PIQUANT PHRASE, St. Teresa terms mental prayer
the "royal highway to heaven."[1] The thought con-
veyed in her statement is that meditation presents an
easy device for attaining union with God. Again and
again in her writings, St. Teresa pauses to remind us of
the fact that mental prayer quickly raises one to previously unrealized heights of holiness.

It might appear a bit naive to maintain that one single
exercise of the spiritual life can effect so radical a result.
But here again the genius of St. Teresa is demonstrated:
meditation in her concept is *not* a single exercise of the
spiritual life, it is rather a whole new way of living; it
is an introduction into a new life of friendship with
Christ. Her basic definition claims that meditation is
"nothing else than an intimate friendship . . . with

[1] St. Teresa, *Way of Perfection*, xxi.

167

Friendship with Christ

Him."[2] St. Teresa would draw the soul into this friendly contact with Christ and—almost surreptitiously —open to him new vistas and horizons of spiritual living.

When one has begun to meet Christ daily on this level of friendship, his entire relationship to God will undergo a revolutionary alteration. Christ will no longer be a historical figure who lived some two thousand years ago. He will, instead, be a living, personal, knowable friend. And once a person arrives at a practical realization that Christ is not just *something* but rather *someone*, his whole life will be reorganized. Religion for him will not consist in a series of "thou shalt" and "thou shalt not"; no, it will be an exciting, absorbing friendship with Christ. This is the road St. Teresa invites us to travel by engaging in mental prayer.

The beauty of Teresian meditation lies in the fact that the soul is stripped of the protection of formal prayers and thrust into immediate contact with Our Lord. We all know too well that we can ramble through long periods of vocal prayer without ever once meeting Christ directly. And words—words without interior conviction —avail little in our friendship with Christ. Shakespeare so aptly portrays that truth in his *Hamlet*:

> My words fly up my thoughts remain below;
> Words without thoughts never to heaven go.[3]

But was not this the complaint of Our Lord Himself?:

---

[2] St. Teresa, *Life*, viii.
[3] William Shakespeare, *Hamlet*, Act III, scene 3.

This people honors me with their lips but their heart is far from me.[4]

True mental prayer obviates this difficulty by turning the soul squarely into the presence of Christ and leaving him there to fend for himself. There are no standardized formulae of prayer to hide behind; he is forced to speak directly to his Divine Friend.

St. Teresa, after treating of the basic nature of prayer, cries out to Christ:

> I cannot conceive, my Creator, why the whole world does not strive to draw near Thee in this intimate friendship.[5]

St. Teresa's perplexity is understandable: mental prayer offers such vast possibilities in the spiritual life that it is astounding so few people meditate faithfully.

Much of the diffidence in undertaking meditation is occasioned by the initial difficulties experienced therein. Meditation is a new, unique manner of praying for many, and consequently there must be a strenuous period of adjustment. The labor and effort required frighten many. St. Teresa comments on these early struggles:

> Since I am speaking of the first efforts of those souls who are resolved to pursue the conquest of such a great good and come out victorious from their enterprise, I wish to remark to them that the rudest trials are at the beginning.[6]

The most difficult trials are at the beginning—how true! But once the soul has mastered a few of the funda-

---

[4] Matthew, 15, 8.
[5] St. Teresa, *Life*, viii.
[6] *Ibid.*, xi.

mental concepts of meditation, all will be easier. If only the soul can rise over and above these inaugural problems. Accordingly, St. Teresa bolsters up her beginner at prayer with an appeal to courage:

> It is a great mercy on the part of God to give to a person the grace and an energetic resolution to tend with all his strength to perfection by means of mental prayer. Let him but persevere and God who refuses nobody will gradually augment his courage so that he will in the end gain the victory.[7]

Courage, for a little while, and soon one will develop that ease and facility at mental prayer which will make it all seem worthwhile.

Some three hundred and fifty years ago St. Francis de Sales sadly grieved that meditation is a neglected art:

> But perhaps . . . you know not how to pray mentally, for it is a thing with which few in our age are so happy as to be acquainted.[8]

It is a complaint that could be registered in our own times, too. So many omit meditation from their lives on one pretext or another—no one of them valid. By so doing they thereby exclude themselves from the happiness and beneficial results derived from meditation.

St. Teresa, therefore, extends to all a fervent plea and invitation to incorporate the practice of mental prayer in their lives. And if we follow her suggestion, our whole life—not just our prayer life—will assume a rich, vibrant

---

[7] *Ibid.*
[8] St. Francis de Sales, *Introduction to a Devout Life*, II, 2.

tone; we will be absorbed in a close, personal friendship with Christ; we will begin to experience here on earth some of heaven's joys.

Yes, St. Teresa was right: meditation is the "royal highway to heaven."